Inside
Corporate
America

Inside Corporate America

A Guide for African Americans

Wilson Simmons III

A PERIGEE BOOK

A Perigee Book
Published by The Berkley Publishing Group
200 Madison Avenue
New York, NY 10016

Copyright © 1996 by Wilson Simmons.
Book design by Rhea Braunstein
Cover design by James R. Harris
Author photograph by Judge Dixon

First edition: February 1996

Published simultaneously in Canada.

The Putnam Berkley World Wide Web site address is
http://www.berkley.com

Library of Congress Cataloging-in-Publication Data
Simmons, Wilson.
Inside corporate America : a guide for African Americans /
Wilson Simmons III.—1st ed.
p.   cm.
"A Perigee book."
ISBN 0–399–51983–1
1. Vocational guidance—United States.
2. Afro-Americans—Employment.
3. Afro-American executives.
4. Career development—United States.   I. Title.
HF5382.5.U5S49   1996
331.7'02'08996073—dc20   95–23050 CIP

PRINTED IN THE UNITED STATES OF AMERICA

10   9   8   7   6   5   4   3   2   1

331.702
S592

To my mother,
Mae Jacquet-Simmons

CONTENTS

Part II: Making the Team

Part III: Survival Is More Than Instinct

ACKNOWLEDGMENTS

To: Irene Prokop, Deb Louis, Judge Dixon,
Sam Donato, David Skolnick, Joe Louis,
Bronda Everett and Larry Williams.
Thank you.

INTRODUCTION

❖

If we stand tall it is because we stand on the
backs of those who came before us.
—YORUBA PROVERB

While living in Philadelphia, near the art museum, and working as an account executive for Levi Strauss & Co., an unexpected encounter completely altered the way I looked at myself in the larger cosmic scheme of things. On a crowded bus on the way to a meeting at Strawbridge & Clothiers, the most prestigious department store in Philadelphia, dressed in my best navy blue suit, I was steadying myself on the overhead metal handle when an elderly black man touched me on my shoulder. I responded with a smile and a "Yes, sir?" He said, "Young man, you make me real proud. You are what we worked so hard for." I replied with a very humble "Thank you," not really knowing what to say to this. His eyes shone with this wonderful sense of pride, and I was too moved to say anything else.

Why this elderly black man picked me out of all those people on the bus to speak to is still a mystery to me. And it continues to have an impact on me. Getting off the bus, I made a beeline to the nearest phone and called my mother at home in Los Angeles. While telling her the story, I started crying. That was in 1981 and until this day it is still a story that I can't tell without having to stop to get myself together. That day my focus changed to one of having a responsibility *as a black man*. It stopped being about my BMW or the kind of bindings that were on my skis.

After I graduated from college, my desire was to teach high school and coach football in the same community of Compton, California, where I grew up. I was in college when President John F. Kennedy was shot, and I was in the Army stationed at Fort Bragg, North Carolina, with orders to go to Vietnam, when Dr. Martin Luther King, Jr., was killed. In the sixties, with my brothers and sisters in college, I pledged that we would take the word to our brothers and sisters in the streets who were not as fortunate as ourselves. I sat on the floor of a classroom at San Jose State and listened to Stokely Carmichael talk about black people working together as a people and how it would be nonsensical to do otherwise. I listened in Los Angeles as Maulana Karenga said, "Black people should band together, because if we don't we will die alone, and as a monument to our ignorance maybe the white boy will put our head on the nickel like he did the Indian." I had never taken those messages in as part of who I was until a little old black man tapped me on the shoulder.

With twenty years in corporate America, working for companies like Polaroid Corporation, the 3M Company, Levi Strauss & Co., the Los Angeles Clippers, and the United Negro College Fund, a motivating factor in the writing of this book was my lack of access to the "good ol' boys' network" while employed with Hallmark Cards. In retrospect, this is not surprising, given the racial dynamics of America in 1972. Out of the hundred or so Hallmark businesspeople on the West Coast, not one was black. There was no one I felt comfortable enough to approach and ask for help. This book is about how to get inside the doors of corporate America, and how to be successful in what will in many cases be hostile situations.

It is one thing to approach a job with enthusiasm and optimism, and it's something completely different to be naive. Corporate America has rules and everybody plays by them. As in any other human enterprise, the rules are made by the ruler. Since the head man is generally a white man, you have to expect a great deal of favoritism toward his own kind in the tilt of the playing field. This book will tell you as African Americans how to get in the door, and what to expect once you step across the threshold.

This book is not about the racism that exists in corporate America, because that is no revelation. Unless you've been off the planet for some time, you know that racism is alive and well in America. It's just my own story of surviving and succeeding. The information in this book is not about some theory based on a number of people interviewed. It's real and I know it works because I've done it. In my research of books on interviewing and being interviewed, I found that most writers/authors are experts only by association. Imagine telling someone how to be a major league batter without the benefit of ever having batted against major league pitching yourself. I am certain there is room for argument in that analogy, but ponder for a minute getting hit with a baseball going a hundred miles an hour. You have to question whether your batting instructor can help you unravel the mental part of getting back up to bat.

I am grateful to that wonderful elderly black man in

Philadelphia, because he engendered in me the burning passion to write this book. It is only now after much prodding from family and friends, that I decided to . . . Just Do It.

> *Success is a journey, not a destination.*
> —BEN SWEETLAND

PART I

◆

Inside the Doors
of Corporate America

SUCCESS

To laugh often and much;

to win the respect of intelligent people and
the affection of children;

to earn the appreciation of honest critics and
endure the betrayal of false friends;

to appreciate beauty;

to find the best in others;

to leave the world a bit better, whether by
a healthy child, a garden patch or a redeemed
social condition;

to know even one life has breathed easier
because
you have lived.

This is to have succeeded.

—RALPH WALDO EMERSON

1

Ten Important First Steps

The will to win is important,
but the will to prepare is vital.
—JOE PATERNO

The steps up to the doors of corporate America will put you to the test. To begin with, the employment status of young African Americans is pretty bleak. We represent 15 percent of the population as a whole, according to the census count. Yet we are 33 percent of the welfare population, which is more than double the number of African Americans in college. The statistics make you realize we must do whatever is necessary to help one another.

Much of the information that bombards you about getting a job is a waste of time. The job hunting process is precise, not the enormous numbers game suggested by many. For instance, sending five hundred resumes out to different companies is a crap shoot. Yet many young men and women do it every year, hoping someone will pick their resume out of the bunch. My personal experience is that you will have a better shot at winning the lottery. And buying a lottery ticket is less expensive.

Most job hunters are not sophisticated enough to adjust

their resumes to the requirements of specific jobs, and most companies throw away resumes that don't fit their job specifications. In today's job market, you have to think like an employer, entrepreneur and profit center. You have to understand both the product line and the goals of the organization and you have to demonstrate that you can effectively and cost-efficiently contribute to the achievements of those goals. Otherwise, why are you there?

Getting a job is one of the most competitive games around. There are no runners-up, no second chances. So preparing yourself—mentally, physically and emotionally—is not just important. It's vital.

Going to see headhunters (executive search firms) is also a waste of time if you are just graduating from college. Headhunters steal people from other companies (which is why they are called headhunters in the first place), so unless you have been with a company at least two years and are on the fast track, they have no use for you. If a headhunter does have time for you, then you know you are either talking to a rookie or someone who is going to send you off to a company that will beat an unsuspecting recruit to a pulp. After six months of this treatment, you will have absolutely no self-esteem left. To borrow a phrase from one of the top headhunters in the country, "I find people for jobs, not jobs for people." If you are working, and good, they will find you.

Your number one priority is to be face-to-face with a decision maker no matter what line of work you're looking for! The following steps are designed to ensure that you don't appear desperate for a job, even if you are. No one likes a desperate person. Once you are face-to-face, be prepared to be put through the paces. Do not make a big fuss just because you are asked to fill out an application. Fill out the application quickly and completely. Put the pertinent information on a piece of paper beforehand so you won't be fumbling around for twenty minutes looking for names, correct phone numbers, titles for references, dates of hires, and salary history. The only thing that you should have to do is transfer the information to the application form they hand you.

Know from the beginning that a bad attitude can only work against you, and cheerfully accept the rules of the game. Filling out the application is just one of the rules. It is a known trade secret that the interview really begins when you are handed a clipboard, an application and a cheap pen. Don't ever write "see resume" on the application unless you are instructed to do so. To some "see resume" means that you probably don't take direction very well, or you can't be bothered doing repetitive tasks. So prepare yourself for the application ordeal.

Anyone you use for a reference should know that you are using his or her name. You don't want any surprises, so make sure you and your references are in tune.

I admit to knowing some white people who have done some pretty crazy things to get a job. Like sending a shoe in the mail, with a note attached saying, "I'll do whatever it takes to get a foot in the door." There are literally hundreds of crazy and desperate ideas to get in the door, and probably one out of a thousand will work. One brother camped out on a president's doorstep to show his determination to work for a company. To his surprise, he was arrested for loitering. Many companies feel, if you're off the wall now what will you be like once you are hired? The most effective ways to job search are to apply directly to the employer, or to go through friends, relatives, and acquaintances, which are personal referrals. Less than 10 percent of successful job hunters find those jobs through newspaper ads or with placement services. This relates to the fact that only one out of every five available jobs is ever posted anywhere.

Your chances for success, then, are improved when you are willing to prepare. Consider looking for a job as a full-time effort, which it is. There are no shortcuts—if there were, I would have found them by now. My brothers and sisters, once you realize the challenge, here is how it's done . . .

1. RESEARCH

Researching the company you are going to interview with is of paramount importance, and if you don't do it, you position yourself as a passive rather than an active interviewee. The result: You will be fielding questions for the better part of an hour, while trying to avoid mistakes. Obviously, when you've researched a company, you have made the commitment to make a job happen, and you can begin to interview the interviewer (step 9). For now, research is the most important first step you can take.

Often an executive recruiter will have a brochure on a particular company for you to read. You have to know that the brochure is the company's best foot. You want to dig deeper. After all, this is your career. The library is the most reliable source of information. Check *Standard and Poor's Register of Corporations, Directors and Executives, Dun and Bradstreet's Directory,* Moody's manuals, and a business periodicals index. If you have a personal computer with a modem, there are a few online services that are useful for researching, such as Prodigy, America Online, and CompuServe.

Call up everyone you know who may assist you in doing your own background check of the company. Or contact someone who is presently employed by the company with whom you are interviewing. Ask what it's like to work for the company. You will be surprised at the information you will receive, and how much more comfortable you will feel about interviewing.

Your research should familiarize you with the company's plans, profits, products and the number of minority employees (if any). So much information is available you will be tempted to memorize it. Don't. Note highlights on a three-by-five card and use it as a reference to review periodically before your actual interview. You should know the names and titles of key players you may meet. But always remember, when in doubt throw out the R.O.P.E.:

- Research the company
- Organize your time
- Prepare by role-playing
- Enthusiasm covers many mistakes

THE RUSE

Many times you will have to call a company to get the necessary information to plan your strategy or to send your resume. In sales, this is known as a "cold call" because you have to pick up the phone, or visit a client whom you've never spoken with or seen before. In business, mastering the cold call is mandatory. The following sample dialogue is one way to obtain information and practice the cold call. "Good morning, who would I talk to about getting information about your company?" (You will generally be talking to a receptionist or a secretary, and they are programmed to say: "Who's calling please?") "My name is [whatever it is] and I am a student at [name a school close by], and I have been assigned to research [name of company] for my marketing class. Can you mail me some information on your company?"

That is generally enough to get all the information that you need. Everyone loves to help students. I was still using the student ruse ten years out of college. If you want to know the specific name and title of someone, just ask and you will get it.

2. THE RESUME AND COVER LETTER

Your resume should be on white paper with black ink. Colored papers and parchment only cost you money. Your resume should be one page in length. If you can afford to have it done professionally, do so. Otherwise use a model in one of the many handbooks for this purpose in your local library, and have it laser printed.

Do not put references, race, place of birth, height, weight, religion, date of birth, citizenship, or health on your resume. None of this information is relevant until you are face-to-face. Then you will have plenty of time to divulge more about yourself. If you are face-to-face with an employer, most of this information will be on the application you filled out. Keep in mind, however, that it is illegal to require any job applicant to supply religion, race, age, or marital status.

There are certain choice items on your resume that corporate America loves: career-related affiliations, corporate internships, campus organizations (varsity sports, fraternities, sororities, campus political organizations), work experience, military experience, and the willingness to relocate.

You can also vary the size of the typefaces in printing your resume, for headings such as Objectives, Work Experience, Education, and Personal Data, to make that piece of paper as presentable and professional as possible. But remember, your resume is just a tool to get you in the door. Ultimately *you* will be the one they hire, *not* the words on your resume. The resume is just part of corporate America's game, and one of the keys is that it be visually appealing and that it fit the specifications of the job. Many recruiters will take a resume and rearrange the information to fit the job description each time you apply for a job.

Do not put down a degree unless you have one, and be prepared to support all claims in the interview. The urge to inflate job responsibilities and titles on the resume can be overwhelming, particularly if your experience is entry level. After all, you want to present a broad enough base of skills to attract the eye of an employer, but you don't want to be caught like a deer in the headlights when you are asked a specific question for which you have no answer.

Your resume should be accompanied by a cover letter stating your intention and marketing your potential. The following letters are good examples of appropriate cover letters.

IF YOU ARE JUST ENTERING THE JOB MARKET . . .

Dear . . .

Your write-up in *Adweek* magazine about the introduction of your new line of tennis shoes was quite intriguing. Frankly, I think the idea is not only fashion forward, but what the market has needed for some time.

I am in my junior year of college at [name of college] studying business with an emphasis on marketing and have spent my last two summers working in sales of athletic wear. As a college athlete, I am familiar with the trends and needs of today's athletic consumer.

I will be in the Los Angeles area for the spring break and would like to poke my head in the door to discuss working as an intern for you this summer. As you will note on my resume, I have a good combination of sales and marketing experience. Looking forward to meeting with you.

Sincerely . . .

WHEN ASKED TO SUBMIT A RESUME . . .

Dear . . .

As per our conversation, I am sending you a copy of my resume. As I briefly mentioned over the telephone [when we met, etc.], I have [however many] years of experience in several areas of marketing and promotion that could be useful to your organization. [Or I believe my education has been perfectly suited to an XYZ corporate entry-level position.]

I would like to meet with you to discuss present or future positions in person. Thank you.

Very truly yours . . .

IF YOU ARE LOOKING TO CHANGE JOBS . . .

Dear . . .

I am writing to you because I believe I can make a significant contribution to the overall future growth of [name of company]. Throughout my career, I have demonstrated my abilities in sales and marketing and proven myself as a skilled administrator. With [however many] years of hands-on experience, I have successfully increased sales through innovative marketing programs. This proven success in generating productivity came about primarily because I remain completely aware of all situations involving [type of product] and stay in line with marketing programs that drive sales.

I am a person with a high degree of self-motivation, leadership ability, and an understanding of the need to interact successfully with all levels of personnel. The enclosed resume will illustrate my ability to handle the rigors of sales in the corporate arena. May I suggest an early telephone contact to arrange a meeting for the purpose of exploring our mutual interest?

Sincerely . . .

WHEN ANSWERING AN AD . . .

Dear . . .

I am very interested in the supervisory position that you advertised in the *New York Times* on May 23, 1995.

My background has been in management and supervision, including my own business and experience as supervisor of a department of the New York Transportation System.

I have enclosed my resume and letters of recommendation to give you additional information about myself.

I would appreciate an interview to talk about this position. Please call me at [your number] or write to me at my address below. Thank you.

Sincerely . . .

In writing cover letters to employers, never write "To whom it may concern." You want to send your resume to someone who has the power to hire you. And "To whom it may concern" is likely to mean the circular file. When you write someone's name, then someone is accountable for some type of response. You will have one hell of a time trying to follow up on "To whom it may concern."

Also, *never, never, ever* start a letter with "Dear Sir . . ." With more and more women moving into executive positions, you have a fifty-fifty chance of killing yourself off before your letter is even read. One executive consultant of the female persuasion that I know said point-blank, "If they're stupid enough to assume that a man is in this position in this day and age, I don't want them working for me!"

You should also know the person's appropriate title. For tips to obtain such information, see The Ruse, page 9.

3. AFFIRMATIONS AND RELAXATION TECHNIQUES

An affirmation is a positive statement which declares something to be true. Affirmations will program info into your subconscious mind that you are the right person for the job. Write on a piece of paper exactly how you want to appear in front of an interviewer. Just by writing it out, you will program yourself to be confident, relaxed, and poised. Your affirmation should read something like this: "I, Carter Woodson, will be poised, confident, and relaxed when I meet with Elijah McCoy on January 18, at 10:30 A.M. My preparation, knowledge, and ability to perform the job will be evident to Mr. McCoy. I trust my feelings and support them. I tune into what I want and act on it."

Affirmations are very powerful and help counteract any negative feelings or beliefs you might have. Review your affirmation at least twice daily to ensure the proper mindset. If you don't say these affirmations about yourself, you're cheating yourself out of a powerful ally: your inner mind. Every major religion, twelve-step program, and self-help course utilizes some form of affirmation, because they work. Whatever passes thy lips, so too shall you be. Repeat the affirmation out loud at least twice a day.

To program your body to relax and appear confident, practice relaxation techniques. One such technique is meditation. You should sit or lie in a comfortable position. Close your eyes and relax. Take several slow, deep breaths, relaxing your body more deeply with each breath. Count to ten each time you inhale, then count again as you exhale. Release and relax your mind and do the same for your body. Imagine that your body is sinking through the floor. From this relaxed position, imagine yourself working for the company that you have been researching. Imagine that you are being congratulated for the wonderful job you have been doing. Imagine the job as being fun and fulfilling for you. You feel relaxed, energized, and powerful. You are successful at what you are doing because it is exactly what you want to be doing.

Do this exercise on a daily basis, and it will get you in touch with that part of yourself that wants to be expressed in this way. Also practice the deep breathing before you go into the interview.

To really prime yourself for the interview process, start with companies that give the mirror test. The mirror test refers to placing a mirror under your nose to see that you are breathing. In other words, companies that use the mirror test interview and hire anyone. Copier companies, insurance companies, recruiting firms, and cellular telephone operations are just a few. These types of companies are really great to interview with because they traditionally look for the hard-driving employee. And if you interview well with these types of companies, you are well on your way to getting the job you want.

One caveat: actually working for these companies is not for amateurs or the weak at heart. Maybe one out of ten employees make it in the business. Most are on commission with some type of draw. So you may only want to use them as a training ground to interview; however, keep in mind that the one of ten who succeed in mirror test companies make a very nice living for themselves.

4. YOUR BODY

Successful people have one look in common: the glow. The glow is that fresh look on your face you receive from exercising, and exercise can be had for free. If you are not exercising, then you are eliminating one of the key elements to a great interview. Being physically fit enhances both your listening and verbal skills. Your energy will not only be apparent in your voice but in your face as well, and enthusiasm will be very difficult for the interviewer to overlook. Many people in the movie industry describe this glow as "having presence."

You should exercise at least four times a week. If you exercise for thirty minutes on a stationary bike four times per week, you will have the glow. If you exercise more, and you already have your own regimen, then you are that much better off. But the absolute minimum is four times a week.

Your diet is also a key. Without going into a dissertation on proper eating, you should avoid eating candy, sweets, and fried foods. Start eating vegetables, fruits, and hot cereals. On the morning of the interview, try to eat eggs, which are touted as helping your metabolism function efficiently, and are the recommended breakfast food for students taking tests.

An interview will end in many cases if a candidate starts talking about health problems, so leave yours at home. Interviewers are not only biased against color but weight as well. If you are overweight and all things are equal in terms of education and experience, you are more than likely to lose out to someone that is more proportionate in weight and height. That is a serious reality check. How will you answer the question: How is your health?

As African Americans, we have grooming situations that are unique to us. For a black woman, the hair is going to make a statement about her. And since styles vary from close cropped to braids, the issue is one of compromise. What is the culture of the company in which you are interviewing? What style are the women of color there wearing? It's a sure bet that it's conservative. With the unlikelihood of braids being a part of the corporate culture in the near future, it would be prudent to eliminate braids or dreads as your style. Of course, if freedom of personal expression is important to you, chances are you aren't going to interview with ultraconservative companies. But, again, keep in mind that the first thought an interviewer has is how well you will fit into the company profile. Don't let outrageous hairstyles work against you. Men leave the designer lines and extreme fades with your barber.

One of the most neglected parts of the body is the hands. Hands are very important, not only because we use them to express ourselves, but because they tell the interviewer about our hygiene. Well-groomed hands are a must. If you have acrylic- or silk-wrapped nails, wear a

French manicure or clear polish. Long nails are out. Efficient, neat nails are short and clean, for men and women. Your hands also serve one very important function at the interview: They deliver the handshake. For better or worse, the handshake creates part of your first impression and is the focus of the corporate greeting ritual. Shake hands crisply, firmly, and with one squeeze. Don't pump up and down or use both hands. Wait for the interviewer to offer a hand first, but if it isn't forthcoming, offer yours. Never begin an important meeting without shaking hands.

Facial hair is probably the toughest test for a black man, because shaving can be a nightmare, but other than a neat mustache, the rest of your facial hair must go—at least until you get the job.

5. DRESS FOR MEN

Too many people approach interviews as a time to make a fashion statement. To resist the temptation to be fashionable, think of your suit as a uniform, because that's exactly what it is. The Magic Suit is a two-piece single-breasted navy blue suit. I emphasize single-breasted because a double-breasted suit can be cumbersome, and a three-piece suit is far too pretentious. Most people who wear double-breasted suits to an interview are not sure if they are supposed to unbutton the suit or keep it buttoned when they sit. Most double-breasted suits have three buttons, which is too many buttons to deal with. So don't wear a double-breasted suit.

Don't put anything in the pockets of your suit. It should be freshly pressed. Cuffs on your suit pants are optional, through they make the pants hang better by adding weight to the bottoms. Your pants should be long enough to "break" gently over the shoes. Socks should not show when you stand up. Off-the-rack doesn't mean fits-like-a-sack, so look for the best tailoring and proper fit before you purchase a suit.

A white long-sleeved dress shirt is another part of the uniform. Not blue, beige, or striped, but white—only. Be sure it is professionally laundered with starch. Do not wear cuff links or monograms; button-down collars are optional. Wear black shoes freshly polished, and black socks. No rings unless it's your wedding band, no pins, or earrings; in fact, exclude jewelry completely.

The tie allows for some flexibility but not very much. Red, burgundy, or blue will do; just remember that the companies that you will be interviewing with are conservative, so don't try to impress with that $100 tie you got for graduation. If you are not sure about the color of the tie, check out the men who work at your local bank, or look at photos of corporate executives in *Forbes* or *Black Enterprise* magazine.

Carry a briefcase if you own a good, conservative one, and in it have a copy of your resume, as well as something to read if you are kept waiting. Newspapers are messy, but the latest issue of *Business Week, Time,* or *Ebony* is appropriate.

6. DRESS FOR WOMEN

Guidelines for women's dress varies from industry to industry, so it is important to pay attention to detail. You should know what the dress code of the company is that you are visiting. Unlike men, women are allowed some creativity in their dress, but not very much. There are still some guidelines and they are conservative, so refrain from making a fashion statement. It is recommended that you wear a suit to an interview, in navy blue or gray, with a long-sleeved white blouse. The front-tie bow is still one of the favorite looks, even though I hear women complaining about feeling like a flight attendant. It is also acceptable to wear a brown or black suit, and the blouse can be gray or beige, but it is not wise to stray too far away from the conservative look. Think uniform. And avoid low-cut necklines, tank tops, or T-shirts, no matter how cutting-edge the company. The cut of your suit can be avant-garde, but it must still convey a conservative image. Be sure your skirt is also of conservative length. Check it when you sit to see if it reveals too much leg or thigh. Leave slit skirts at home, with long, flowing ones and minis.

Shoes for women should either be black or navy with closed toe and heel. Avoid heels higher than an inch and a half, and never wear sandals. Stockings should be flesh tone, or a soft shade of your suit, but not jet black or opaque tights. Hosiery should never draw attention away from what you are wearing. Be sure to put an extra pair of stockings in your briefcase. It is impossible to be confident in an interview and have a gigantic run up your leg, so be prepared.

Don't carry both briefcase and purse to the interview. Put a small clutch in your briefcase along with that extra pair of stockings, a copy of your resume, and reading material in case you are asked to wait.

Excessive jewelry is out. Don't wear rings unless it's a wedding or engagement ring. Earrings should be small and in good taste. Bracelets for the wrist and ankles are not necessary, and distract you and the interviewer. A rule of thumb is: if it dangles, jangles, swings, droops, wiggles, shines, glitters, or clanks, don't wear it!

7. INTERVIEWS

Unless you know someone, or have relatives inside the doors of corporate America, you must go through the arduous task of interviewing for the few remaining job openings. Even if you do have a contact, chances are you're going to need to interview with someone else anyway. I honestly don't know any brothers or sisters who are in a position to say, "Hire him/her," but if you follow the steps that I've listed, your chances are as good as any and better than most to get the job you want. I consider myself an expert at interviewing—no brag, just fact. Take it from me, interviewing is an art form from beginning to end. But it is an art form you can learn.

The most important part of interviewing is mind-set. You should have your script down so pat that no matter what they throw at you, you can handle it. You must present a fine balance between being able to talk about yourself and yet not be too long-winded. No answer should be longer than sixty seconds, but must be to the point, which means giving specific answers. This is not a time to be humble, so you should have three to five outstanding relevant achievements which you can include in your answer to the question "Tell me a little bit about yourself."

Your posture is vitally important. Body language lets the interviewer know if you are really interested in the job. Never sit back in the chair, and never cross your legs. Maintain eye contact, as well as a keen interest in what the interviewer is saying. Sit forward in the chair, and if it is at all possible, sit next to the interviewer. Your posture should say that you are listening to every word that he or she is saying.

Don't smoke, chew gum, or drink anything. Simply decline all invitations to smoke or drink by saying, "No, thank you." Never look at your watch, or the clock on the wall. Never read anything on the interviewer's desk. Never interrupt the interviewer. (Believe me, that takes a lot of practice.) Being late all but knocks you out of the running for a job. The truth is, there are no excuses for being late.

Address the interviewer by his or her last name, unless you are told to do otherwise. Always give your first and last name with a smile and a firm handshake. Show some enthusiasm. Employers really do look for bright, assertive go-getters who'll get the job done.

Strategy in the interview is so crucial that I've likened it to football, because in daily life, football is the closest thing to war. You must think like a warrior. As in football, the best offense is a great defense. In an interview, as long as you are answering questions, you are on defense. Fortunately for you, corporate America has been running the same offense for the last twenty years, so you have the opportunity to anticipate its every move in advance. (See Questions and Answers, below.)

On occasion, an interview might be held by a potential employer at lunch or dinner. Do not mistake this for a social occasion. Do not forget for a second that you are being studied, observed, and evaluated. One of the most frequent errors job candidates make is to let their guard down, especially when asked to share a meal. Instead of behaving with civility, etiquette, and decorum, they have a major mental lapse and become theatrical, believing they've been invited to perform. During a lunch or dinner interview, keep these points in mind:

- Do not forget why you've been invited.
- Do not drink alcohol or smoke at meals, even if invited to do so.
- Do not take medicine or drink milk in front of the host; he or she may think you suffer from stomach problems.
- Do not raise business matters before the host does.
- Do not order messy foods, like spaghetti.
- Do not speak with your mouth full.
- Do not joke with restaurant personnel.
- Do not complain about anything.
- Do not reach for the check or decide when to leave. Such prerogatives belong to the host.
- Do not forget why you were invited.

8. THE QUESTIONS AND ANSWERS

To prepare your offense, and develop a positive mind-set, here are some questions most frequently asked by corporate America, as well as the responses they most favor.

Question: What type of position are you interested in?

Gail Blake Smith (Pacific Bell) said what concerns her more than anything is when a candidate says, "I'm interested in an entry-level position that will enable me to learn this business inside and out and will give me an opportunity to grow." Her feeling is if they don't know *which* entry-level position they are interested in, they haven't done their homework. Again, research is vital, so your response should be:

Answer: I am interested in your management training program because it will enable me to learn this business inside and out.

Being specific puts you ahead of the parade of candidates interviewing at the same company.

Now what if the interviewer responds with something like: "We don't have any openings in management training." or, "Why such an unusual area?" which could be tricky—especially if you are a woman applying for a position in a typically male field. Your responses, then, should be positive and will once again rely on your research. Do not slump in your seat and assume the interview is over. Instead, answer with your own question, repeating your goals: Well, I'm interested in learning the company inside and out. If there are no current openings in management training, where would you suggest I start? Often an interviewer will say there are no openings in order to see how adaptable, and how determined you are. Throw the ball back by asking for an alternative spot. After all, you want to appear determined to get the job. In the case of the second question, restate your goals, look the interviewer in the eye, and respond: I am interested in learning about the company from the ground up and I believe this is the best position in which to start. Do you disagree?

By asking the last question, you may cause the interviewer to admit that yes, it is the best position, or to fumble with words like "But it's not typically a position for women," or men, or people of color. If you experience the fumble, continue with your interview as planned. Do not get defensive, but make a mental note and refer to it when you are offered the job. Discrimination is everywhere, but you don't have to buy into it by working for someone who is only out to fill affirmative action requirements.

Question: Why do you think you would like working here? Or, What do you know about our company?

If you have done the necessary research, this is a slam dunk. If I didn't get this question from the interviewer, I would prompt him or her with the following statement:

Answer: I am very impressed with the company and the challenge the position presents.

Now you have set up your next play, for questions dealing with the company or type of work.

Question: Can you take direction, orders, or instructions?

Answer: This was always an easy one for me because I would always say, Yes, as a Vietnam veteran with an honorable discharge, I have no problem taking orders. End of story.

If you have played varsity sports, or have been a part of any organization that requires that you follow some direction or instruction, use it. Say I have absolutely no problem taking direction, I am a team player, and I will do whatever is necessary to get a job done.

Remember, many questions are designed to see how you think on your feet. Because truly, "can you take direction?" is a rather stupid question, topped only by "Are you looking for a permanent job?" If you are going through this process, then you are looking for a career. Think *career* and you will not be trapped with trick questions.

Question: What is your greatest strength?

Answer: My strengths are being persistent, competitive, persuasive, and doing whatever is necessary to be the best. I am also goal-oriented and very much a team player.

Question: What is your biggest weakness?

Answer: (pick one): (1) I sometimes become so involved in my work that I lose track of time. (2) I demand a great deal of myself and sometimes become impatient with people who do not make equal demands of themselves. (3) I work very hard and sometimes get impatient with people who do not work hard. (4) I have sometimes been called a perfectionist, because I demand a lot, not only of myself, but also of those who work with me.

Your answer must be safe, going from a perceived negative to a positive. The workaholic syndrome is a good image to project at this point.

Question: Where do you want to be in three to five years?

Answer: I am very goal-oriented. If successful, how far can I go?

As before, don't worry about answering a question with a question. Unless you know exactly *where* you want to be in three to five years, and *why* you want to be there, you set yourself up to be knocked out of the box. If you do know where you want to be, then say so: "Paul, in three years, I would like to be a sales manager. That would allow me to utilize my people and organizational skills." If you do specify a position you'd like to achieve, make sure you know something about it.

Question: Would you say there was any racial prejudice at your last company?

Answer: I certainly would like to think not.

This has to be one of the most frequently asked questions of people of color. The answer diffuses the question and by its nature suggests that you are on a higher plane. The tone of your voice should suggest surprise to such a question. In reality you want to say, "New to the planet, are you?"

Question: Why are you leaving your present company?

Answer: "When I researched the background of XYZ company and the growth opportunity, I didn't see how I could refrain from meeting with you." If you are going through a headhunter you say, "I received this call from Lewis Latimer and when he explained the background of your situation and the position, I didn't see how I could decline this opportunity to meet with you."

Never bad-mouth your company, no matter how poorly you may have been treated. Avoid race questions like the plague—they're a trap. No one likes bad news. Never say you were fired, even if true. Suggest a staff cutback, layoff, company reorganizing, or leaving by mutual agreement.

Question: How long would it take for you to make a contribution to the company?

Answer: I'm a quick study and I understand the business, so I anticipate making a contribution almost immediately.

Question: What do you think of your previous boss?

Answer: I learned a great deal from Marcus, my manager at ABC company. Now I feel the need to explore my full potential in the job market for growth opportunities.

Never trash your boss or company. Remember, you are positive, upbeat, goal-oriented. There is no room in your mind-set for negativity.

Question: Why should we hire you?

Answer: I've researched XYZ company and know XYZ by reputation. My background fits perfectly with the corporate culture. It appears to be a great match and would probably result in a long-term relationship.

Question: What compensation are you looking for?

Answer: Well, Paul, you certainly know more about me than before we met, and I certainly know more about the opportunity we've been discussing, and frankly, I am very interested and confident I can do an outstanding job for you, and I am confident you would make me a fair and reasonable offer.

This answer is one you want to memorize. The answer lets the interviewer know that you're interested and confident, and that you have sized up the company as a fair one. It also helps keep you from underpricing yourself, which is a temptation, especially with first jobs. Remember, you are worthy of a good career and the compensation that comes with it.

DIRTY TRICKS

Many employers will play games with your head just to see how you think on your feet. A friend of mine tells the story of a man in his firm who is six-foot-five and interviews prospective candidates for the company. One of his favorite exercises is to watch to see if a candidate matches his stride as he walks to his office. He doesn't hire "laggers."

I could give you a hundred questions and not cover all the questions companies will ask. Some companies ask bizarre questions and some love brain teasers like "Why are manhole covers round?" (Answer: If they were square, they could fall down the hole.) Have fun and learn from the experience. If you have practiced your affirmations and psyched yourself up for the interview game, trick questions—dirty or otherwise—won't throw you. Instead, you'll be able to keep your balance and show the interviewer you can handle a rebound.

9. INTERVIEW THE INTERVIEWER

Listening plays as big a part as asking the questions. You don't want to be so programmed that you ask a question that has already been answered. If you are just starting out, you want to ask: Why is this position available? What's an average day like? What's the future of the company? (You better have a good idea before you ask this question.) What type of orientation program do you have? Who are your closest competitors? What is your ranking in the industry? You are obviously very successful, how did you get to the position you are in today? (People love to talk about themselves.)

All these questions must be asked with feeling. Practice the questions on friends and family (role-playing). If you are at all halfhearted in any part of the interview, you will just be wasting your time. My favorite two questions are: If I were to come aboard next Monday morning, what would be the first thing you would want me to direct my attention to? Second priority? (The answer ends up in most cases being the job description.) *The second question is the most important, because it's asking for the job—an absolute must to get into corporate America:* Paul, I have learned a lot more about the company, and you have learned a lot more about me—is there anything in my background or experience that would prevent me from getting this outstanding opportunity? When you ask this question, *shut up*—you have just closed. *The name of the game is to get an offer.* This close will work for even the crusty old pro. Don't let the interviewer off the hook—if her or she starts dancing, close again. You might hear "I am seeing a lot of people so I am not making a decision now." You say, "Paul, if you were making a decision today, where would I stand?" *Shut up*—listen to the answer. If you don't hear a yes, ask: What are your reservations?

Bonus Question: Paul, if you were me with my background and experience, would you accept this position if it were offered to you and if so, why? *Shut up*—listen to the answer. If he sells you on the job, extend your hand, look him right in the eye, and say: "You know I agree with you for all of those same reasons—is Monday a good starting date or would Tuesday be better?"

Never ever say: "I hope to hear from you." Remember, *closing is asking for the job,* and that's an absolute must.

If you don't ask for what you want in corporate America, you'll be sure not to get it.

10. THANK-YOU NOTES

Each person who grants you an interview deserves a thank-you note. It is absolutely crucial that you mail a note that very night to anyone you talked to that day. It costs very little and the result will mean a great deal in your moving in the right direction of getting the job that you want. A thank-you note is regarded as basic to the simplest dictates of courtesy. After all, you are presenting yourself as someone who has the ability to treat people properly. Prove it. Your actions must be consistent with your words. The note also helps them remember you.

Sending a thank-you note is one of the most overlooked steps in the entire process of getting a job. This is not an optional amenity. It is critical. Make sure you get a business card from everyone you meet, so that you will know where to send the thank-you notes.

An appropriate thank-you note should be typed on white or buff letterhead (your own) with the same heading and typeface you used on your resume. It should read something like this:

Dear . . .

Thanks so much for the opportunity to meet with you on Friday, March 31, 1995, to discuss the position in Marketing as assistant product manager of XYZ company. It's an exciting opportunity, and I am looking forward to hearing your decision very soon.

Sincerely . . .

Dear . . .

It was indeed a pleasure to meet with you on Thursday, to discuss the opening in your sales department for sales manager with ABC company. The climate is undoubtedly one in which I can make a significant contribution almost immediately.

I have been considering other situations, but I have postponed the decision until I hear from you. Your prompt reply would be greatly appreciated.

Sincerely . . .

TIPS FROM THE PROS

MICHAEL THOMPSON, POLAROID CORPORATION

If you just graduated from college, where would you look for a job?

I would not take a resume and make a lot of copies and send them off to a bunch of companies. I would be very focused. I would identify four corporations where I felt my skills base could match up with their needs. After I had established who these four corporations were, I'd do a lot of work in terms of getting background on these corporations and it would be fairly deep. I'd go places like CompuServe, or the library, and get Info Track, and I would research all of what the companies are about. Everything from its bottom line to its balance sheet. And I would look at its strategic direction and initiative. From there I would take a very focused direction in terms of communicating to these businesses—why my skills would enhance their business in terms of bottom-line performance, reducing risk, and increasing revenues.

That would be my approach. In short, I would not use a shotgun, I would use a rifle.

What do you look for in a job?

First of all, I look for a challenge. I look for fun. I know most people don't think of jobs in terms of fun. I look for a job where I can make a significant contribution. Ideally, it is my feeling that opportunities for blacks are in jobs that have a lot of growth in them. This means not necessarily looking at businesses within a corporation that represent the core of business, or a maturing business. I've always felt I like to roll the dice. In the past, I've worked with a lot of what would be considered starters, taking an entrepreneurial approach to doing the business. You find that within companies, too.

If I was not a part of a corporation and I was looking at a corporation, one of the first things I would look for as an African American person is, what kind of diversity program do they have in place? Because if you get hired by a company and they don't have a real commitment to diversity, then you're going to be the kind of guy that sits by the door. The old token brother of the sixties and seventies. And you're going to be frustrated in a very short while. And you're going to be very lonely.

I'd also look for a company that's got a good balance sheet, because in today's environment, companies are always laying off. So you want to look at companies that have a healthy performance over a sustained period of time, not just one or two good years of performance. I'd look at the industry that the company is in and how they measure up in that industry. In other words, if I were looking at the steel industry and there were four companies, I would probably be focused on the number one or two companies. I certainly would not want to look below that. In addition, I would look at a company in terms of what its commitment to the overall aggregate community is—that is, its environment, how they treat their people. I would talk to people who have worked for that company and I would talk to people who they do business with.

Finally—I know a lot of people might have trouble with this—when I approach a job, I look at it as if I may be doing the job for the rest of my life. So I want to assess it in terms of, can this job or will this job challenge me? And I say you should do that whether you are going to be there for six months or six years.

RHONDA WINDHAM, PUBLIC RELATIONS AND
PROMOTIONS, LOS ANGELES LAKERS

What are some of the mistakes brothers and sisters make in the interviewing process?
I think people go into interviews only thinking about their own accomplishments. It's important to be prepared. Research the company. Find out what has made them successful; how they started; how much money they make; what is the five-year plan of the company.

GAIL BLAKE SMITH, PACIFIC BELL

What are some of the mistakes brothers and sisters make in the interviewing process?
Not knowing what their agenda is. They are not sure, even though they have had four or five years of college to address a career and hopefully get prepared for it. Most of them have no clue. They are just looking for a job. Pacific Bell is looking for people who are career-oriented. It is exceedingly expensive to train someone just for the initial job. We are looking for people who are going to stay, so that we can get our return. People coming in are not up to even playing the game. It's a game. Most don't know how to market themselves. They have no idea of what they want to

do in the short-term future. Let alone the long-term. I always ask, why do you think we should hire you? They seldom know anything about the company that they are interviewing with. There are very few that call in advance and say: Send me your annual report. Seldom do they concerns themselves with what our strategic goals are. They just don't do their research. And it is apparent in the interview.

You're not going to get a second chance to make a good first impression. I know I, like most people, discern within twenty minutes if I am going to see this person again.

JIM CHITTY, BAXTER HEALTH CARE

What are some of the mistakes brothers and sisters make in the interviewing process?

The most common mistake a brother or sister makes in the process is when a brother walks into an interview situation and the interviewer is a minority person. The brother or sister will tend to relax. He will say something like, "Hey, what's happenin', blood, what's up?" And that's the biggest mistake that a candidate can make. You don't know that person. A black person is not from one mold. He's going to expect the same behavior, the same respect, the same dignity, the same responses, that you will give to the white interviewer.

In my experience, sometimes the brothers are a lot harder on minority candidates than they are on white candidates, usually because they wonder who's watching them. If they hire someone who is black and they fail, they're disappointed. And it might make somebody think they don't know what they're doing. Sometimes they see inadequacies in themselves, and they think people are watching. If you hire a white candidate and he fails, it's no skin off your back. So sometimes brothers doing interviewing have their problems, too. You have to walk in and just carry through with the same game plan that you prepared no matter who that person is interviewing you.

Secondly, I think we make the same mistake in reverse when we're dealing with white human resources people or interviewers. It's very important that something about you personally bleeds from the interview. I think it's important that you be yourself in many ways, because it's going to come out if you get hired. It's probably going to come out in the interview, too, because there will be a lack of consistency. If you play bid whist and not golf, say it and be proud of it. The interviewer is looking for people who are honest, and I think most people can see when a person is doing a fine acting job.

So be cautious when you go into an interview. Ignore the interviewer's race, and age, and whatever, and just do the best possible job.

BERNARD KINSEY, CONSULTANT, CORPORATE AMERICA'S CEO'S/PRESIDENTS & VP'S

If you just graduated from college, where would you look for a job?

I'm not sure if I were graduating from college now that I would even look for a job. I think particularly for young black people I would ask them to look for business opportunities where they can not only look for a job but could end up owning businesses and employing people themselves. It seems to me that the real opportunities are in young people and old people, really . . . finding needs that have not been met by products and services and creating that kind of product, and then marketing it back to the people who have demonstrated a need. It seems to me that everywhere you look there are people that made money hand over fist doing this. You got Bill Gates, who decided that an operating system for a new PC would be a new invention. You got the guy Ellison with Oracle— these are all billionaires. But you have regular guys that have done extremely well over the years. Everybody cannot be an entrepreneur, so what I would suggest . . . if you are going to look for a job, I would ask myself where the trends are for the next ten to fifteen years. Psychologists and behaviorists say now that the average person graduating from college today has about a 25 percent chance of being unemployed. The average college graduate working will have seven to eight careers before they die. Which means that in our generation we could look to two, two and a half careers before we die. So what you have to say is that you do not belong to a company, and a company does not belong to you. What you want from a company is skills and employability. What you need to do is to take the opportunities that the companies give you and be able to apply them in many varied ways. It's sort of like what aerospace engineers have done for years. Aerospace engineers never worked for McDonnell Douglas or Boeing, they really worked as engineers. They were aeronautical engineers to the extent that people began to think about aerospace engineers moving from Seattle to Los Angeles and vice versa . . . or to Wichita, Kansas, and think nothing of it, because they wanted to pursue their profession. And I think that's what most people have to begin to look to the future for.

What are some of the mistakes brothers and sisters make in the interviewing process?
There are a lot of mistakes to interviewing, and there's really no common answer to a good or bad interview. But

what I look for and talk to people about is being yourself. I think the best quality that you can project is the quality that is you. And being honest about what you deliver and really anticipating what job you are going for and what kind of questions that may be asked. I know when I go in to talk to a company (as a consultant) I get their annual report before I go in and see them. I find out where the president, CEO, and the executive VP (which is the level that I deal with), went to school, and what they did and how they got there, and what kind of products and services they provide, and find out what their hot buttons are. So that it's really a two-way street. And I've always felt that no one was interviewing Bernard Kinsey as much as I was interviewing them. Because I felt that I was always a pretty hot ticket. And I felt that they had to come across my scale, as much as I had to come across their scale. And to the extent that you are really on top of your game . . . I think that this is a key point . . . in the twenty-five years I was in America's corporations, I never interviewed for a job after my initial job with Xerox. I worked for Xerox for twenty years, ten years as the vice president. I got promoted every eighteen months for twenty years. When you have the kind of qualities that people see and want, they come to you and offer you jobs. You don't have to go seeking them out. There are a lot of ways to do that; that's just something to keep in the back of your mind.

JOHN KELLY, PRESIDENT/CEO, ENTERPRISE NATIONAL BANK, LANDOVER, MARYLAND

If you just graduated from college, where would you look for a job?

A recent college graduate should seek employment opportunities where they can learn the most and have the most favorable opportunity for job satisfaction. When you first enter the world of work as a professional, it is good to already have made an assessment of your expectations for yourself and your employer. For instance, is money more important than job challenge? Do I want to sacrifice geographic preference for future opportunities for growth in the company? Once you've identified your critical needs and expectations, you are ready to research the industry of your choice, and pursue the job that is right for you.

What do you look for in a job?

As a career banker, I've always looked for a challenging, stimulating position that recognizes my ability to bring something important to the position. Financial security is important, but it has never been at the top of my job satisfaction priority list. Working long hours to achieve a goal is second nature to me. I enjoy new and innovative job environments and I've held positions within the banking industry that satisfied my needs for recognition and achievement.

What are some of the mistakes brothers and sisters make in the interviewing process?

The interviewing process is fundamental, and rarely requires altering as you go from one industry to the next. In banking, the employer is looking for a certain type of individual, depending upon the position being filled. Whether interviewing for a management position, or entry level, it is always good to follow some basic rules:

1. Dress for success. Wear the appropriate attire that they expect for the position.
2. Be yourself. The interview will go well if you re-

lax, be confident in what you want to say, and convey your expectations of what you are seeking from employment with the company.

3. Talk about your strengths, but don't ignore your weaknesses if asked. Questions like "What would you say are your strengths and your weaknesses" should be answered honestly. A laundry list of your accomplishments followed by a response like "I really don't think I have any weaknesses" is not believable.

4. Don't be afraid of asking questions about the job, the business, and what the employer's expectations of a new employee are. An applicant who is interested in what the employer's needs are shows maturity, a highly motivated individual, and someone who is interested in a particular company, not just there because they need a job.

5. Above all, answer the questions on the application honestly, concisely, and completely. Don't just skip obvious questions such as your high school education because you have a resume to leave with the interviewer. *Don't scratch out!!* Be neat—it's the only picture the employment interviewer has of you when you leave.

PAT WATTS, SOUTHERN CALIFORNIA EDISON

If you just graduated from college, where would you look for a job?
Private industry, governmental agencies, nonprofit organizations, educational institutions.

What do you look for in a job?
Challenge, opportunity for advancement, personal satisfaction.

What are some of the mistakes brothers and sisters make in in the interviewing process?

Lack of confidence, inability to show critical thinking skills; oftentimes they do not research the job before the interview and therefore are not aware of what skills are being sought after.

WILLIAM BURTIES, ASSISTANT VICE PRESIDENT,
UNION BANK

What are some of the mistakes brothers and sisters make in the interviewing process?

Brothers and sisters sometimes make the mistake of not dressing to the image they need to portray. The biggest mistake that I see in the banking industry is that they seldom do any research. We are an international bank and soon to be one of the largest banks in the world, and yet many of the applicants think that we are local. Make sure you know why you want the job.

2

Selecting the Right Company

*You cannot fight by being on the outside complaining
and whining. You have to get inside to be able
to assess their strengths and weaknesses
and then move in.*
—SHIRLEY CHISOLM

Because a career takes up a very large portion of your life,
selecting the right company is very important. You can
interview with many companies and take the first job offered, but you can empower yourself by coming as close
as you can to getting the job that you want. If this doesn't
happen the first time, be sure it happens with subsequent
jobs by researching more thoroughly and preparing yourself more fully.

Many companies have training programs, and they are
known throughout the business industry as the best companies to learn from. As an example, Procter & Gamble
(P&G) is a corporation with an excellent training program. They are the classic packaged goods company, and
you will learn more in their training program than you
will in any MBA program. On the other hand, a company
such as the Polaroid Corporation has no real training program. Almost everyone who works for Polaroid either has
some experience with a competitor or comes from a com-

pany like P&G, so movement in these corporations is common.

Also, the consumer industry is changing fast. It won't be long before corporate America makes some drastic changes in its hiring practices, and that's good news for people of color. It was not long ago that corporate America had the mistaken impression that African Americans could not be corporate spokespeople because they couldn't sell products. Yet Michael Jordan, Bill Cosby, Whitney Houston, Diahann Carroll, and several other athletes and entertainers are selling millions of dollars' worth of products every year. Michael Jordan alone can be credited with Nike's capturing about 28.4 percent of the market for athletic shoes sold in the United States. Nike spent some $50 million to penetrate the European market coinciding with the 1992 Summer Olympics, with Michael Jordan in 75 percent of the ads.

Athletic shoe companies, clothing companies, electronic equipment companies, packaged goods companies, beverage companies, and entertainment-related companies all use spokespersons and it won't be long before our brothers and sisters who are out front speaking for these companies begin to ask: Why don't you have some brothers and sisters working for you? Your job, my brother and sister, is to be in the position to take advantage of opportunities that will become available. If you are in college, you should write to some of these companies (a list follows this chapter) and let them know you would like to intern for them. If you are a college graduate, apply for a full-time position. Even high school is not too early to start inquiring and researching. We have a big plus on our side: *We are hungry!*

There are four key areas that you should consider in your selection of a company:

1. TRAINING PROGRAMS

If you are going to make a career in corporate America, your best start would be a company with a training program. The time invested will follow you throughout your career, and it will be useful if it is necessary to go from one company to another. There are no schools that will teach what you will learn from companies that have training programs.

One thing that remains constant among most corporations with training programs is that you must be willing to relocate to a designated assignment after completion. Training is one of the largest investments companies will make in you, and there is no guarantee that they will get a return on their investment. The company, as a rule, will pay the cost of your moving.

Hallmark Cards has one of the most extensive training programs in the industry. The training is hands-on, and you are actually assigned to a prescribed trainer. Hallmark sells products and services to retailers in card shops, department stores, chain drugstores, supermarkets, and mass merchandise outlets. The emphasis in the training is a thorough understanding of all business products, with effective retail management skills.

Know when you interview if there is a training program and ask to be a part of it.

2. INTERNSHIPS

Being an intern for a company gives you a pretty good idea what the corporate culture is all about. You will have a chance to see from the inside what the job actually entails. From the outside, some jobs seem to be pretty glamorous, but once you're on the inside the true picture is anything but. Although being an intern is a thankless job, it is one of the best investments that you can make in your career.

There are so many ways to describe being an intern: gofer, flunky, servant, underling, peon. You are like the water boy, or someone who launders the team's uniforms. Although your position is peripheral, you are being studied for team membership. In any case, it is the best way to get in the door. And in many industries, it is the rite of passage that you intern before you do anything with the company. The thinking is that you should learn from the bottom up. At least that's what they say. The truth is, it's basic training (boot camp) all over again.

Interning for a company may mean having to give up your summer, or it may mean working part-time during the school year. Some companies pay a salary, but most don't. The market is so competitive now that you almost need to do some interning to get a leg up. It is the only way to gain firsthand knowledge and experience. You will have an opportunity to compare academic theories with actual work situations. You'll develop professional references and enhance your job search qualifications. You will have the chance to meet many corporate executives, and work in many different departments. Ultimately, you'll have a better idea of what to look for in a permanent position.

While working for Levi Strauss & Co. in Chicago in 1980, my daily routine included picking up cigarettes, fetching coffee for managers, cleaning showrooms, and doing odd jobs in the office. And this was after eight years of experience in marketing and sales. The routine was performed by everyone in the Chicago office who was waiting for a permanent assignment. In the entertainment industry, your first step is the mail room. In publishing, it might be as a receptionist.

Later in my career with Levi Strauss, a young woman working for me part-time expressed an interest in employment with the company. She had the responsibility of doing my inventory counts in the department stores in Philadelphia and New York, and had two years of college. At the time, Levi was looking for an intern. I explained that if she did exactly what I told her to do, she would work for the company sooner than she thought. I prepared her for the interview, explaining that it was going to be the easy part.

The tough part was going to be to get an assignment in the children's wear division. The strategy was that she would work in the New York office as a person of perpetual motion. No one should ever have to wonder what she was doing. I told her to take only a thirty-minute lunch, and to take that lunch in the lunchroom. She would start at one showroom and work her way around the floor until all the showrooms were neat. She would volunteer to help salesmen in the office on any projects they had. Never complain—just appear as a working machine. More importantly, complete every task asked of her. She did everything she was instructed to do and she received an assignment in upstate New York after only three months. She went from earning $6 an hour to making $65,000 in her first full-time year.

The idea is not so much that you are being a flunky. As I told her, if she cleaned the showrooms and put the swatches on the clothes, she would learn the Levi's children's clothing line and she would know how everything worked so that when the time came to get an assignment, she would be ready. So actually there is a method to the madness. More important, she proved that she was a valuable team player.

Diligence and persistence will pay off in the end, often with surprising benefits.

3. UPWARD MOBILITY

You want to work for a company that allows you to grow with your talent, a company that has a road map to the next position. Marketing and sales are areas where there is tangible evidence of your performance, and where training translates into many other opportunities. You also want to work for a company that will promote you when you have done the job, although there is never any guaranteed promotion. What you want to do is position yourself with a company that has a career development program, and a reputation for promoting employees who are willing to pay the price for success, i.e., work hard and be a team player.

Being in marketing or sales allows you to go in many different directions with a company, and within others. Once you have been with a company for a while, you will have time to structure your own game plan to move up the corporate ladder, or take your skills elsewhere. Your initial concern, however, is ascertaining whether a model for upward mobility is in place or not. This is reason enough to talk to someone of color who is presently working for the company. If all entry-level jobs are dead-end, choose another company and don't think twice about it.

4. MONEY

Don't work only for a company you like. Work for a company that will pay you the big bucks.

Money is the bottom line. It is how we keep score, and the scoreboard never lies. Money is how we identify successful people in our society. It is what makes the environment so competitive. You will never have to look for your numbers, because they will always be in front of you. The scoreboard will be blinking overhead from the time you leave school to the time you leave business.

Be careful when you start looking at a company's entry-level salary offering. Often companies will be short on the front end and big on the back end, once you've moved up.

There are certain companies that pay very little up front, and even sell you against the job. It's called the negative sell, and you will know you're getting the negative sell when you hear about long hours with very little pay. If you have done your homework, you know better.

An example of the low front end is selling radio time or TV time. In the beginning, you make less than $1,000 a month. But by the third year, if you are worth your salt, you will be in the six figures, and that's a fact. So have a short- and long-term goal, then measure potential companies against them.

THE TOP 25 COMPANIES

I recommend these companies for many reasons, but most of all because the training and benefits you receive from them are invaluable for making a career in corporate America. They are all large, national, and receptive to minorities.

1. HALLMARK CARDS, INC.
   College Relations Manager
   PO Box 419580
   Kansas City, Missouri 64141-6580
   (816) 274-5111

A family-owned company that is sensitive to hiring minorities. The company has a no layoff history. There are between twenty to thirty paid internships. You must be a college senior to qualify for an internship. Entry-level positions are available in production, distribution, sales, marketing, and product development. Benefits include medical and dental insurance, profit sharing, and a retirement plan.

2. POLAROID CORPORATION
   549 Technology Square
   Cambridge, Massachusetts 02139
   (617) 577-2000

Polaroid was an early supporter of equal opportunity employment. The products are used in amateur and professional photography, science, medicine, and education. Positions are available in marketing, manufacturing, and sales. Benefits include fully paid disability leave for childbirth, up to six months unpaid parental leave, part-time work, job sharing, profit sharing, and an employee stock ownership plan.

3. SARA LEE CORPORATION
   70 W. Madison
   Chicago, Illinois 60602
   (312) 726-2600

One of the more diverse companies in corporate America. An international food and consumer products company, Sara Lee markets and manufactures "high quality marketing-sensitive" products. Major products include Jimmy Dean sausage, Hillshire Farm meats, Hanes, L'eggs hosiery, Isotoner, and Champion.

4. PROCTER & GAMBLE
   1 Procter & Gamble Plaza
   PO Box 599
   Cincinnati, Ohio 45201
   (513) 983-1100

The best training company for consumer products in the United States. Develops, manufactures, and markets laundry and cleaning products, personal care products, and food and beverage products. Positions in market research, sales management, customer service, brand management, finance, and accounting all require college degrees. P&G, as it is known in the industry, offers a summer internship program. Major products include Tide laundry detergent, Ivory soap, Scope mouthwash, Crest toothpaste, Noxema skin care, Charmin bathroom tissue, Hawaiian Punch beverage, and Pampers diapers. A great company for a career, even better for a stepping stone. You must be willing to relocate.

5. APPLE COMPUTER, INC.
   20525 Mariani Avenue
   Cupertino, California 95014
   (408) 996-1010

Apple has no formal training program. Their desktop publishing and communications products are marketed internationally. You can get inside with the right experience. Apple maintains a job hotline at (408) 974-3010. Faxed resumes are accepted.

Also research the video game industry: Disney/MGM, Sega Genesis, Nintendo, Crystal Dynamics, Electronic Arts, and Atari represent a $10-billion-a-year industry. Very soon the communication networks will connect as one. Right now, they are all like a bunch of blind men feeling their way around an elephant: everybody involved in it has a different idea of what this lucrative beast is, depending on what part of it touches them.

6. THE EQUITABLE
   787 Seventh Avenue
   New York, New York 10019
   (212) 554-1234

Working for an insurance company means you will work either in the home office or in the field. If you are in the field, you will be working in sales. Life insurance has been around a long time, and for a long time salespeople were paid a draw on commissions earned. Now most companies pay you a salary in the $30,000 to

$40,000 range. If you are around for four or more years, you will be in the six figure income range. *Warning:* Working in this industry means having your ankles taped and your chin strap snapped. In other words, the faint of heart need not apply. Another way of putting it is, if you plan to have any time off in your first two years, this is the wrong job for you.

7. ALBERTO CULVER COMPANY
   2525 Armitage Avenue
   Melrose Park, Illinois 60160
   (708) 450-3000

Alberto manufactures and markets toiletries, professional hair care products, and food items. The company is divided into different segments: Domestic Toiletries, Household Grocery, Professional, and International divisions. Major products include VO5 hair care products, Born Free shampoo, Mrs. Dash spice mix, and Sugar Twin sugar substitute. Like many companies in this industry, Alberto has underground hiring practices. They have no intern program, but once you connect you become part of the underground.

8. CHESEBROUGH-POND'S, INC.
   33 Benedict Place
   Greenwich, Connecticut 06836
   (203) 661-2000

Chesebrough-Pond's is a subsidiary of Unilever United States, Inc. They manufacture toiletries, cosmetics, and fragrances. They offer intern programs for college juniors and seniors. They have training programs and they also hire for part-time positions. The benefits include medical, dental, and life insurance, an employee pension plan, a savings plan, tuition assistance, maternity leave, and a well baby plan. Other companies under the Unilever umbrella are Ragu Foods Inc., Calvin Klein Cosmetics Corp., Elizabeth Arden Inc., and Thomas J. Lipton.

9. KIMBERLY-CLARK CORPORATION
   Neenah Operations Headquarters
   401 North Lake Street
   Neenah, Wisconsin 54956
   (414) 721-2000

Excellent company to work for, with paid internship for research and engineering. Must be college seniors to qualify for internship. Entry-level staff are hired for financial, accounting, mechanics, electrical engineering, and chemical positions. Manufacturer of facial and bath tissue, feminine pads, disposable diapers, and paper towels.

10. 3M (MINNESOTA MINING & MANUFACTUR-
    ING)
    3M Center
    St. Paul, Minnesota 55144-1000
    (612) 733-1110

One of the best training programs in corporate America. 3M develops and manufactures more than sixty thousand products for business, industry, government, and consumers. Well-known publicly as the company that makes Scotch tape and Post-it note pads. Very sensitive to hiring minorities and persons with disabilities. It is truly one of the best companies to work for in America.

11. EASTMAN KODAK COMPANY
    343 State Street
    Rochester, New York 14650
    (716) 724-4000

Truly a glamour company in spite of some of the troubles they have had, and are still having. Much more diversified than the consumer image projected. You should know that candidates are lined up around the block to work for them. Apart from the photographic products, Kodak manufactures and markets plastic products, health and beauty products, pharmaceuticals and related products. *Black Enterprise* magazine listed Kodak as one of the fifty best companies for black employees. They are committed as a company to minority recruitment. Major products: Bayer aspirin, d-Con pest control products, Midol, Mop & Glo floor cleaner, batteries, film, Kodak cameras and film processing chemicals.

12. WARNER-LAMBERT COMPANY
    201 Tabor Road
    Morris Plains, New Jersey 07950
    (201) 540-2000

Develops, markets, and manufactures health care and consumer products. Provides a three-month paid internship program for the summer. Major products: Dentyne gum, Certs breath mints, Rolaids, Listerine antiseptic, and Schick shaving products. Benefits include health insurance, sick pay, family leave, and long-term disability. Most of the recruiting for entry-level positions is done on college campuses.

13. COCA-COLA COMPANY
1 Coca-Cola Plaza
Atlanta, Georgia 30313
(404) 676-2121

The largest of the beverage companies, they do a lot of recruiting and are one of the lowest in starting pay. Don't be turned off—what you learn from Coca-Cola may make you a star later. Great things await those who hang around for a while. Benefits include a pension plan, college tuition assistance, and savings and profit sharing plans. In addition to Coca-Cola, some of the company's major products are Hi-C fruit drink, Minute Maid fruit juices and soft drinks, Better-Nut coffee, Sprite soft drink, and Tab soft drink.

14. GENERAL MOTORS CORPORATION
3044 West Grand Boulevard
Detroit, Michigan 48202
(313) 556-5000

Once in this industry, you must know that it is difficult to make the transition to a packaged goods company, but the doors are wide open for the hungry. Benefits include medical, dental, and life insurance. A few of the GM products include Chevrolet motor vehicles, Cadillac and Buick automobiles.

15. HARTMARX CORPORATION
101 North Wacker Drive
Chicago, Illinois 60606
(312) 372-6300

The clothing business is one of the most lucrative positions for businesspeople in the country. It is also one of the hardest industries to crack. I met a Guess? Jeans representative who was making over $200,000 a year, and was complaining because some of the department stores were cutting back. Most of the clothing manufacturers require that you pay all your own expenses. If you are lucky enough to get in, no one will be able to drag you out. Starting positions are usually found in marketing, manufacturing, and sales in the clothing business. Major products are Pierre Cardin, Racquet Club–Wimbledon, Hart Schaffner & Marx, and Christian Dior.

16. GILLETTE COMPANY
    Prudential Tower Building
    Boston, Massachusetts 02199
    (617) 421-7000

Solid company, with an excellent training program. Very sensitive to hiring and promoting minorities. Gillette offers a summer intern program for college seniors. Benefits include college tuition assistance, medical and life insurance, vision insurance, and dental insurance. Some of the major products are Right Guard antiperspirant, Oral-B toothbrushes, Liquid Paper correction fluid, Paper Mate writing instruments, and Foamy shave cream.

17. JOHNSON & JOHNSON
    One Johnson & Johnson Plaza
    New Brunswick, New Jersey 08933
    (201) 524-0400

A company that actually looks for minorities to hire. Although they are very picky, they are not nearly as tough to crack as some of the others. Johnson & Johnson offers paid summer internships for college juniors and seniors. The company accepts unsolicited resumes with cover letters (Attn: Human Resources Department). Some of the major products are Band-Aids, Mylanta, O.B. tampons, Living Rubber gloves, and Shower to Shower body powder.

18. BAXTER INTERNATIONAL INC.
One Baxter Parkway
Deerfield, Illinois 60015
(708) 948-2000

Baxter, which was American Hospital Supply, is just that—a hospital supply company. Once the hospitals started taking precautions because of AIDS, the supply business went through the roof. I know a brother personally who has been earning over six figures for the last ten years. This company has made tremendous efforts to hire minorities.

19. TIME, INC.
Rockefeller Center
New York, New York 10020
(212) 522-2507

If you can get into the magazine industry, get in. It is another one of those tightly knit industries where the openings seem to be passed on to relatives and friends. Someone in sales gets a commission for every ad that you see in a magazine, since magazines survive by ads. They are a magazine's lifeblood. If you have the opportunity to start with a company, don't be turned off by the low starting pay. There is big money to be made. Get in any way you can.

20. McGRAW-HILL, INC.
    1221 Avenue of the Americas
    New York, New York 10020
    (212) 512-4203

Publishing companies are similar to magazines in their hiring practices, but most employees value the family-like atmosphere and flexibility. There is much movement from one publishing house to another, usually for advancement, but often sales reps remain with one particular company throughout their careers.

21. NIKE INC.
    One Bowerman Drive
    Beaverton, Oregon 97005
    (503) 671-6453

Nike is ripe for brothers and sisters who are interested in sports. My counterpart with Levi Strauss in Philadelphia left the company to work for Nike in children's wear (pre–Michael Jordan). He made over $100,000 his first year and had nothing to do with selling tennis shoes. Those guys make $300,000+ a year depending on territory.

Do anything you can to work for Nike, because very few brothers and sisters are inside selling, but the prediction is that this is about to change. Most of the salespeople calling on the big hitters (stores that buy in large volumes) have developed a following. Which amounts to who you know. It's the same song and dance that you will hear when you first start looking for a gig: you're nice, but you don't have any experience. (No kidding, Sherlock, I just got out of college . . .) If it means working at a Foot-Locker during the summer, get some shoe experience, because if you get this gig, you have won the lottery.

It will take energy and willpower to get an interview. Nike ran an ad recently regarding sports participation. It read: "If you couldn't join a team, what would you join? If you couldn't shoot hoops, what would you shoot? If you couldn't dream of touchdowns, what would you dream?" The ad goes on to say, "Participating in sports is no longer a given for young people in America. For some, it's because they can't afford equipment. For others, it's because there's no place to play . . . We believe play is a right, not a privilege. If you agree, please call P.L.A.Y. at 1-800-929-PLAY."

This is an ideal opportunity to let Nike and companies like Nike know that your dream is to work for them. Apart from all the brothers out front representing the company, at this writing Georgetown coach John Thompson is an advisor/consultant for Nike. African-American women should know that these opportunities include them, too. Be as prepared as possible to leap when the opportunity arises. There are twenty paid internships every year.

22. DIGITAL EQUIPMENT CORPORATION
146 Main Street
Maynard, Massachusetts 01754-2571
(508) 493-5111

Digital Equipment is an international supplier of networked computer systems, software, and services. The company has made major contributions of money and equipment to several black colleges, including Howard University and Tuskegee Institute. If you have a background in marketing or engineering, you will want to do your internship at DEC. The internships are nonpaying, but the opportunity is well worth it.

23. LEVI STRAUSS & CO.
    1155 Battery Street
    PO Box 7215
    San Francisco, California 94111
    (415) 544-6000

This company is not only sensitive to hiring minorities, but has more women working on staff than men. They are always listed as one of the best companies to work for in America. The home office in San Francisco looks like a college campus. And you will see many of the employees having lunch outside on the grass. I don't know of another company that has a better internship program than Levi Strauss. The internships are year-round, full- or part-time, and they are paid. They hire people in merchandising, advertising, legal, and marketing. Many of the interns will work for six months. They accept college juniors, seniors, and MBA students. The downside is that everybody and their brother wants to work for them. Levi receives more than a thousand applications for twenty to thirty openings.

24. REEBOK INTERNATIONAL LTD.
    100 Technology Center Drive
    Stoughton, Massachusetts 02072
    (617) 341-5087

Another very hot company. Above the Rim, a subsidiary of Reebok located in San Diego, California, is very big on promotions, concentrating primarily on basketball. No real training program, but a great opportunity if you have some work experience in sales or marketing.

25. PACIFIC BELL
     33 New Montgomery Street #1100
     San Francisco, California 94105
     (916) 972-2119

Entry-level staff are hired for all positions. Because the market is so competitive now, experience will get you in the door. Paid internships are offered.

3

Sports Franchises

Man's mind, once stretched by a new idea, never regains its original dimensions.
—OLIVER WENDELL HOLMES

The strategy to get in the door of a sports franchise is consistent with everything that was said in the first chapter regarding corporate America. The big difference is that professional sports franchises are wide open for both men and women. The Big Three (basketball, baseball, and football) have taken some measures to hire minorities. Employment is attainable, and the pro sports franchises are waiting for you.

Most of the job openings on sports teams are for salespeople. It is the one area you can count on to have yearly turnovers. The reason for salespeople leaving varies from their not wanting to work on commission, to their dislike of spending most of their time on the telephone. After my own season (1990–91) with the Los Angeles Clippers, I developed a better understanding of why there are so few brothers and sisters behind the scenes. The lowdown is this: there are between seven and ten jobs in sales, three in public relations, two in promotion, one in corporate marketing, a corporate sales director, a director of marketing, and a sales manager. The titles vary, but staff and functions are pretty much the same.

Few of these positions are even advertised. Jobs are made available though a network or the "inner circle." (So what's new?)

Once hired, I asked the question: Where are the black people? What I found out was that the Clippers wanted to hire minorities, but they did not know how. The few minority applicants who were interviewed received the negative sell (see chapter 2, page 47). Generally the brothers and sisters who were being interviewed shut down, wanting only to get out of the interview and never return. What goes unspoken is that you will get a draw of $2,000 to $3,000 per month, and, depending on how well the team does, you can make as much as $50,000 a year. And many salespeople make more.

All sports organizations have salespeople. They are called account executives, marketing representatives, or sales representatives. Their primary duties are to sell season tickets and get group sales (see below). Their secondary duties are to attend all home games (working), press conferences, promotions, cheerleading tryouts (honest!), and game-day meetings. The benefits include medical/dental—and a pair of season tickets. Beginning salaries range from $24,000 to $50,000.

At this writing, one area that is wide open is selling season tickets to the minority market. My advice is to call and ask the team of your choice for a media guide. A media guide is a directory of the sports franchise personnel. It will list everyone's title, from player personnel, public relations, marketing, advertising, and sales, to the equipment manager, as well as details about the competing franchises. A media guide will be all the information that you will need for your research of a professional team. And if that's not enough, they have pictures of the entire staff.

Follow up with a request for an interview. If you want to get in the business badly enough, do some interning for free if necessary. All teams need interns. Who can refuse a free work force? Note: There are more women behind the sports franchise scenes than there are people of color.

SEASON TICKETS

The main job of an account executive is to sell season tickets. The success of selling season tickets has more to do with how the team is doing than your selling skills. The exception is the occasional losing team with a cult following. If you can pull that off, you're set for life! Normally, selling season tickets means spending a large portion of your time on the telephone making cold calls.

All clubs do some type of advertising in both print and electronic media. The advertising generates leads to the sales and marketing office, from prospective clients interested in season tickets. If you are working for a club that has a lottery pick in the NBA draft, that will usually have the phones ringing off the hook.

When I started working for the Clippers, they had the number eight pick overall: Bo Kimble of Loyola Marymount University. Loyola is a university located about a mile from the Los Angeles Airport, near the beaches of Playa Del Rey. There was a great deal of attention directed toward the university because of the unfortunate death on the basketball court of Bo Kimble's teammate and friend, Hank Gathers. Bo Kimble is a six-foot-five guard who led the nation in scoring as a senior with 35.3 points per game while leading Loyola Marymount to the NCAA quarter-finals.

The lottery pick of a local star was responsible for the phones ringing constantly with people wanting to buy season tickets. The salespeople in the office were making as much as $200 per sale. With the furor, many salespeople were making ten sales a day. Everyone in the office was making money—all you had to do was answer the phone. The 1990–91 season for the Los Angeles Clippers was their best ever. Nothing beats having someone call in asking to buy!

Once the excitement died down, it was back to the phones making cold calls. You make at least eighty calls a day and the result is that you make sales. I trained two salespeople that came after the furor, both recent college graduates with no sales experience. The simple formula I presented to them was to make eighty calls a day. Not one less. Though both were new, at the end of the month they were both on top of the leader board.

GROUP SALES

Your second line of responsibility in a sports franchise is getting group sales. Selling to groups is a big part of the business for professional sports. There is a discount for organizations that buy groups of tickets. There are several organizations that participate in group sales, particularly the nonprofit organizations. The club will provide you with leads to make group sales, or you can generate the leads on your own.

I was fortunate to put together a couple of large group sales. One of the group sales strategies was "Gospel Night." Gospel Night had been somewhat of a tradition with the Clippers. So it was no surprise when I was given the assignment of pulling it off. The tradition had been that the Clippers used an outside source to gather choirs from the local churches in the community.

The great thing about this was that it allowed me to go into the community and sell the Los Angeles Clippers. You will find that the black community as a whole is wide open not only to group sales but to season tickets as well. Very little effort had been made to go into the community. (No mystery!) I decided that it would be appropriate to add a little twist to the traditional Gospel Night by including the Martin Luther King, Jr./Drew Medical Center in the event. So the event was billed as Gospel Night, with the funds going to the children with sickle cell disease at the King/ Drew Medical Center. This automatically involved the community, and actively engaged the hospital in selling the tickets.

Kenneth Hahn, who was the supervisor (2nd District, Los Angeles), became involved in the event because the hospital was in his district. Caffie Greene, who was on the board at the hospital, was responsible for recruiting Danny Bakewell of the Brotherhood Crusade to provide the buses. A partial list of people attending represented the community: Walt Hazzard (former NBA star), Whitman Mayo (actor), Linda Ferguson (president, Young Black Scholars), Rev. Chip Murray (First AME choir), Reggie Smith (LA Dodgers batting instructor), and the bottom line is that the hospital made good money from the event, and I sold my quota of seats.

The truth is most clubs do good business in group sales, unless you are the Chicago Bulls. Successful clubs that sell most of their seats for season tickets will not have room for group sales, but very few teams enjoy that position.

If you love sports, you will have a lot of fun working with sports franchises, and when you work for a professional sports organization, doors open easily. Careers in sports can range from ABC Sports, ESPN, and Nike, to *Sports Illustrated* magazine and so on. The opportunities abound.

GETTING PROMOTED

The NBA headquarters in New York does a lot of hiring from NBA teams around the league. If you are performing a function well for the team you are working for, you have a chance of going to the Big Apple to work. As elsewhere in corporate America, if you get a good offer, you make the move. There are several areas that I suggest you research in addition to the NBA itself: NBA Entertainment, NBA International, and NBA Properties. All these groups have large public relations, marketing, finance, legal, licensing, and media divisions. There are more than three hundred jobs in The Tower (Olympic Tower, NBA Headquarters).

While working for the Clippers, Randy Hersh was promoted from director of marketing to a division of the NBA called Team Services, as the team services manager. To take the mystery out of the job that she left as director of marketing: some of the responsibilities included booking halftime entertainment, recruiting someone to sing the national anthem, developing promotional ideas to include sponsors (time-outs), coordinating dance team routines, and timing everything to coordinate with league guidelines.

When the club hired coach Larry Brown, I decided to check out his debut in his first game against Houston. For the halftime entertainment, the director of marketing (who will go nameless) booked someone to perform with Hula Hoops. Los Angeles is the entertainment capital of the world. It's Hollywood! For goodness' sake, you could go down to Venice Beach and get entertainment better than Hula Hoops for *nothing*. Yet someone paid a man to twirl hoops for ten minutes. My reason for pointing this out is that they are not hiring geniuses, regardless of how high powered the title sounds! Once you're inside, carve out your niche and go for it.

While you will find a complete directory of sports organizations in the Appendix, a few merit some special comment:

PRO BASKETBALL

ATLANTA HAWKS

The only professional sports franchise whose behind-the-scenes personnel is reflective of the product presented on the court. The only other sports franchise that comes close is the Atlanta Braves. Henry Aaron is very outspoken about pro sports including people of color.

PHOENIX SUNS

Owner Jerry Colangelo has endorsed an organization called Sports Careers. If you are interested in a career in sports, this company will put you in a bank of resumes for about $250, which is a crap shoot at best. But the idea represents the enormous interest in the sports world. They are going out of the way especially looking for qualified minority women.

BASEBALL

LOS ANGELES DODGERS

The Los Angeles Dodgers are listed as one of the most desirable organizations to work for. Four free tickets to every game, profit sharing, beautiful corporate headquarters, and among the best places to work for minorities. Listed as one of the one hundred best companies to work for in America.

ST. LOUIS CARDINALS

Board Chairman August Busch also owns Anheuser-Busch, which sponsors the annual Lou Rawls Parade of Stars Telethon to benefit the United Negro College Fund.

PART II

Making the Team

RULES OF THE GAME

Genuine wisdom is usually conspicuous
through modesty and silence.

Do not follow where the path may lead. Go
instead where there is no path and
leave a trail.

Faith is the element, the chemical which,
when mixed with prayer, gives one direct
communication with infinite intelligence.

Our lives can be an accident or an adventure.
The choice is ours.

Desire, when harnessed, is power. Failure to
follow desire, to do what you want to do
most, paves the way to mediocrity.

Ninety-nine percent of winning is being
positive and excited.

The man who believes he can do something is
probably right and so is the man who
believes he can't.

Don't wait for your ship to come in, swim
out to it.

4

Sales Training,
Even If You Aren't in Sales

*To effectively communicate, we must realize that
we are all different in the way we perceive the world
and use this understanding as a guide to our
communication with others.*
—ANTHONY ROBBINS

This will be one of the more vital sections of the book, because we all sell something at one time or another. All life is about selling, be it an idea, service, or product. The days of the salesperson wearing the white belt and white shoes is gone forever. They don't even refer to the position as that of salesperson anymore. Now it's marketing representative, account executive, marketing manager—and these people don't sell. They are in the business of solving problems and building businesses. In fact, every person in business needs to solve problems, manage people, and handle confrontation.

If you decide that advertising, public relations, marketing, manufacturing, or production is the business arena that you are interested in, you are still going to need to understand sales and its dynamics. The first and the toughest test will be when you interview. Because you are selling yourself. Once you become a part of the corporate team, at some time you will be asked to make a presentation (sell an idea) to a group of businesspeople. Today's corporate America has started trimming the fat, and they will be doing so well into the twenty-first century. Cronyism, nepotism, favoritism, and the good ol' boy network are on the decline, being replaced by professionals who are committed to making things happen.

PROBLEM SOLVING

In order for you to make things happen, you must be a problem solver. The key to success is building relationships. Master the art of being a problem solver and the sky will be the limit for you as a professional. Throughout this book, I talk about listening and asking questions. To be a top producer in any industry, you will have to perfect those two skills. Many businesspeople push products without even considering the customer's needs, wants, or problems. Many investment bankers and stockbrokers do the same. Look at what happened in Orange County, California. The person you are dealing with should feel you have his or her best interests at heart.

A problem solver is seldom considered a salesperson, but instead becomes a partner in the customer's business. So conversations are about increased revenues, merchandising, co-op advertising, promotions, and profit margins. You can go to all the sales training courses in America, and learn every close that has ever been used, but none of that will be nearly as important as the skills you develop as a problem solver. I have taken several business courses over the years. Companies either have their own in-house training program or they employ some outside source to teach you. And it still gets down to perfecting the skill of asking questions and listening.

ASKING QUESTIONS

In order to be a problem solver, you are going to have to ask a lot of questions—after all, you can't solve a problem unless you know what the problem is!

Before you start asking questions, it helps to ask for permission. Often, people won't open up unless they understand why you are inquiring about their situation, needs, and problems. My approach has been to tell the person why I want to ask some questions and then, in a very low-key manner, ask for permission. For example:

- "Ms. Tubman, so that I can understand exactly what you are looking for, I'd like to ask you a few questions. OK?"
- "Mr. DuSable, I believe that I have something here that can be of considerable value to you. To be sure that I understand your unique situation, may I ask you a few questions?"
- "Mr. Latimer, I know you have a meeting in just thirty minutes. It would save us some time if I could just ask you a few questions to get the big picture, OK?"

Once you have the OK to go on, ask easy questions and work your way to the more revealing questions so that you can uncover the client or colleague's needs and desires. Concentrate on what the person is saying, so that you can get the whole picture instead of a little piece here and a little piece there.

When you ask questions, you are in control. Just ask any lawyer! Who? What? When? Where? and How? remain the cornerstones of key questions. Regardless of how cantankerous or hostile people may be, psychologists point out that asking sincere questions will not increase their anger. Instead, the right questions will disarm them quickly.

The secret is to keep asking questions until the other person has nothing more to criticize or complain about. To keep the information flowing, never interrupt or attempt to refute a statement. Wait until the other person has said all there is to say. Research shows this is the precise moment when other people, in spite of their attitude, will be most receptive to your position. Here are some illustrations that show how the power of questions can turn problems around, make confrontations work for you, and make you look more graceful throughout the process:

1. *Encourage people to open up.* Some businesspeople are extremely tight-lipped; however, you can usually draw them out with a series of questions.
2. *Discover attitudes.* When you need to know how others feel or what they believe, ask questions such as "Why do you feel that way?" But never, ever discuss religion or politics with a customer, client, or colleague. These are danger zones, and no-win situations.
3. *Keep to the topic at hand.* Whenever a response is irrelevant, ask such questions as "How does that relate to inventory?" or "In what way does that affect your decision?"
4. *Direct the conversation.* When asked for advice, opinions, or suggestions, most people never realize that they have lost control, nor do they suspect that your series of questions can lead them into talking about almost anything you wish to have

discussed. Directing the conversation gives you control of any meeting.

5. *Respond to insults.* While we have come a long way since Jackie Robinson broke the color line in baseball, if you are insulted, resist the urge to fight back. Pause a moment, look the other person in the eye, and say, "I want to make sure I didn't misunderstand. Please repeat what you just said." This is generally enough to disarm the offender.

6. *Confirm questionable information.* Never presume guilt. Always leave room for possible misunderstandings. Ask, "Do I hear you saying something different from what you said earlier?"

7. *Require support for charges.* Rather than trying to justify your position, use questions to put the burden of proof on the customer or client. Ask, "Why do you feel the company is wrong?" or "What facts do you have to support your accusation?"

8. *Simplify meanings.* Never accept implications, vague references, or hints. "When you say you're satisfied with 3M's photographic chemistry, does that mean you've had no trouble with it?"

There are two kinds of questions: open-ended and close-ended. Close-ended questions can usually be answered quickly with a one- or two-word answer, such as, "Martin, are your stores open on Saturdays?" or "Who is the president of your company?" Open-ended questions require more thought and elicit more information, such as, "Why are your offices closed on Saturdays?" or "Why did you suddenly move the Hallmark books to the back of the store?" Armed with these two tools and the following tips, you can stay in charge of any conversation or confrontation, and everyone involved will feel as if he won.

HANDLING CONFRONTATION

1. *Get the facts.* Never jump to conclusions. Use questions to find out exactly what is on the person's mind.

2. *Start with easy questions.* If you open the conversation by asking tough questions or sensitive questions, the other person is likely to be turned off. People open up to questions they know they can answer. So start slowly, even if it means spending a little time discussing unimportant issues.

3. *Be cool.* Keep your voice soft. Keep yourself under control. Never ask questions that are certain to threaten or embarrass the customer, client, or colleague.

4. *Preface questions with facts.* Let the other person know what your perspective is. When you give a little, you usually get a lot more back.

5. *Be concise with your questions.* Be direct and to the point. By piling on many subquestions, you might let the customer evade the most important issue.

6. *When you ask a question, shut up!* No one will ever get angry with you for being quiet while they are collecting their thoughts. The silence in most cases will work for you. It creates an invisible force compelling the other person to answer. Never be the first to break that silence. To quote J. Douglas Edwards, the world-famous sales trainer, "The first one that talks loses."

7. *Let the other person know you listened.* Repeat a few key words, paraphrase, or make a summary statement. Your response in no way means you

agree or disagree. It does encourage the other person to continue talking.

You do not necessarily have to take an aggressive stand to have your point of view understood and accepted by others. Gentle, clever questioning will lead the other person happily to your conclusions.

The business approach I like best for asking questions and gathering information came from my friend Bill Dent in San Francisco. I worked for Bill in marketing the 3M Company's graphic arts and chemistry film to distribution companies in the Bay Area. Bill said, "A businessperson should approach problem solving like the family doctor. That is, rather than going in and trying to sell someone on the features, advantages, and benefits of your product, idea, or service, you should find out what *their* real needs are first." For example, if you were to see a doctor, he/she would not take out the medical bag and throw it on a desk and say, "Take something—I'm sure one of these pills will help you." No, first the doctor will ask, "What's wrong? When did you first start feeling bad? Where does it hurt? How long has it been hurting?" (while taking your temperature and blood pressure). The doctor will ask questions and narrow your ailment down to the best of his/her ability, until he/she can focus on your specific problem. Then, based on training and experience, the doctor will prescribe the treatment most likely to have the best results. The doctor is the gatherer of information.

People open up in response to easy questions because they know that they can answer them, and tough, insensitive questions turn people off. If you ask someone if he has a business partner, he will likely respond with "None of your business." But if you really wanted that information, you could start with "How did you get started in the business?" The easy questions will give you all the answers, because they encourage people to open up. This is beneficial in all walks of life, and in all career arenas.

HOW TO SELL ANYTHING

One thing about sales is that everyone has an opinion on how it should be done. If you listen to everyone out there, you will be totally confused about how to conduct business. Something as simple as selling should not be complicated. And it's not. If you have made it past the interview process to work for a company, you can sell anything. If you are presently working anywhere in corporate America, you already have the ability to be as successful as you wish to be, because the toughest sale you will ever make as a black man or woman will be to sell yourself to corporate America.

Seventy-five percent of all the sales training available on the market today is just fluff. More commonly known as bells and whistles. It's like the extra chrome on a car—it's nice but it doesn't make the car run any better. If you approach the marketplace with the same intensity necessary to get inside the doors in the first place, selling will be the least of your problems. The temptation is to relax once you become comfortable with the routine of the job. How many times can you reinvent the wheel? What you have is a thousand different people saying the same thing. How many ways can you phrase the same question? How many ways can you create the scenario for the importance of listening?

Truth is, you could actually skip all the closes and can all the questions, throw out all those beautiful listening skills, and still be a top-notch salesperson if you just showed up every time you said you would. I think Woody

Allen coined the phrase "Eighty percent of success is showing up."

DOG AND PONY SHOWS

There will come a time when you will have to make a presentation to a group of people. The type of group is as varied as the type of products or information available. Speaking to a group is always a unique experience. You will hear people refer to a presentation to a group as "the dog and pony show."

As part of the newly developed Graphic Arts Team in San Francisco, I was called upon to demonstrate new products to distributors who actually were responsible for selling our product to the end users. You generally have only one shot at presenting new products to a distributor's sales force. You compete with hundreds of other manufacturers for that once-a-week Monday morning sales meeting. You must make the most of your time.

As with any dog and pony show, you become the medicine man or woman, carnival barker, and magician all rolled into one. In a half hour, you have to introduce a new product or idea, simplify the product so that the client will be comfortable in pitching it to end users (newspapers, ad agencies, print shops, etc.), and entertain at the same time. The distributor must perceive the product to be superior, though it may not be. The client or colleague must be persuaded to see it from your point of view, even though it may not be unique. The most important part of the show (aside from the mandatory refreshments) is that everyone must be able to make some money. That's the bottom line.

The dog and pony show should cause your audience to oooh and aaah. It should be entertaining, with some wonderment, and cause your audience to ask questions when you are finished. The difference between you and a magician is that you will share your secret at the end of your show. Which is where the teaching begins. Making presentations has always been a strong point for me because I love doing it. To me, it has always been like being onstage, with the audience giving you immediate feedback.

An example of a dog and pony show occurred when 3M adapted a graphic arts film that was used by everyone in the printing/photographic industry. The twist was that the film had previously been handled under the photographer's red light, and 3M's technology allowed this same film to be handled under a yellow light, with the obvious advantage of being able to see what you were doing much better. So the presentation had to be built around the advantage of using 3M's film as opposed to the competition.

I almost always started off by making fun of myself. My standard, and it has held up for many years, was talking about my brief stint in my own business. You can create your own version of this opening, which will allow you to take control from the jump: "A few years ago, I owned an employment agency in Los Angeles, on Wilshire Boulevard. I was on the twelfth floor of a high-rise building and I was just getting started in the business. My secretary/receptionist hollered into my office that a woman was in the lobby to see me. I asked the secretary to show the woman in. I so badly wanted to impress my first client, I picked up the phone and pretended to be talking to a client. 'Management people? Why of course we have management people! Secretaries? We have a virtual reservoir of secretaries! Lunch Thursday sounds great! No, not this Thursday, next Thursday.' I looked up at the woman standing in front of my desk and asked, 'And what can I do for you?' She said, 'I don't need a job, I'm just here to connect your phone.' " Almost everyone breaks up, and it's then so much easier to go into the presentation.

People love it when you make fun of yourself, which is why so many speakers open with a joke. The attention span of the average person is around seven minutes, however, while I don't find it necessary to be a comedian, I know that you had better be sure you have your audience's attention. I am personally very big on getting volunteers to assist me from my audience.

In demonstrating a new film, I asked a volunteer to read something about the film to our audience. Naturally he had a tough time reading it in the red light. In the meantime, I would develop the film in front of the audience, and switch from the red light to the yellow light while my assistant is still reading. His reading, of course, becomes instantly better in the yellow light. Meanwhile, I am continuing to develop the film before their very eyes. The audience would virtually rush to the table to see the film—with a whole lot of ooohs and aaahs. That, in a nutshell, is your basic dog and pony show. You close by pointing out all the money your audience can make with all the additional incentives the company has dreamed up for whatever the product is. In other words, sell the sizzle, not the steak.

PROMOTIONS (SELLING THE SIZZLE)

The expression "selling the sizzle, not the steak" has been around for a long time. It is the same principle that barbecue joints use in the inner cities of America. You can smell barbecue four blocks from the place, and it entices you to want to eat some. Advertisers do the same thing with selling products.

Lee Iacocca became famous with the Ford Mustang. His ads showed a prim secretary with her hair up, wearing a pair of glasses. The secretary is leaving work, driving to the beach. She takes off her glasses, lets her hair down, and drives to the edge of the water. The top is down on the Mustang and men come running from every direction to surround her car. The commercial gives you the impression that if you buy a Ford Mustang this will happen to you. That ad not only made Mustang one of the most popular cars of all time, it made Iacocca an icon in the world of business.

As you sell, you must think in terms of promotions. What can you do that is different (noticeable)? What makes sense to your customers? There are several ways to promote products. You can be as creative as you wish in your promotions, as long as they sizzle.

CO-OP ADVERTISING

One of the least used and most misunderstood types of promotion is co-op advertising. Co-op ads are generally structured so that the retailer and the manufacturer participate equally in the cost of a particular advertising campaign. Some manufacturers will pay half and some will pay more, but however that is arranged, the manufacturer is a participant in some capacity.

If you walked into a retailer's office and said that you had co-op advertising, you would probably hear something like "So what's new?" But if you came in with a specific plan as to how the retailer can use the co-op ads, and the work was done for them, you'd have the retailer's attention and, in most cases, cooperation.

SELLING THE EVENT

Selling the event is the key to selling the product, because the product is viewed as support for the event. You need only sell your creativity. You become the ad agency, marketing consultant, and salesman all in one. Here's an example.

When I started working for the Polaroid Corporation in Denver, the word from some of my assistants was that I was following a legend. The man that had had the territory left for greener pastures. With Polaroid stock at its all-time low in 1974, and very little margin of profit on Dr. Edwin Land's SX-70 camera, it did not look promising to sell the department stores in the Colorado and New Mexico areas any more cameras. Polaroid was selling these same SX-70 cameras to retailers like Kmart and Target, who are known for "footballing" cameras (kicking prices around) in order to attract customers into the store. This practice was the source of much discussion and bad feeling. Clearly I had my work cut out for me.

On the other hand, department stores can do things on a grand scale. In the Denver area, May D&F and Denver Dry Goods have about thirty stores, with branches all over Colorado. If they decide to promote something, it generally involves all of the stores. Distribution of the SX-70 was sparse in both chains. I made it my goal to get big sales through those stores.

I was told by the camera buyer of the May D&F department store that there was no reason to carry any more cameras than they were already carrying. If someone at a suburban store needed a camera or film, all they needed to do was call the main store and have it shipped in one day. They were not knocking themselves out over the product, because there was a very limited markup on cameras, especially Polaroids. The buyer's feeling was that the SX-70 got the level of attention and distribution warranted by its bottom line. For him, this was the end of the conversation, and the meeting. For me, it was where I started to do my job, i.e., selling.

I explained that I made a living selling Polaroid cameras, and in my view the SX-70 camera was the most innovative camera in the marketplace. I suggested that the store would do well to promote it on a grand scale with large newspaper ads and signs all over the store indicating where customers could find the camera. The buyer wasn't going for any of this, and found a great deal of humor in the suggestion of running an ad in the newspaper.

I asked if, as a matter of courtesy, he would mind if I talked to his boss, to which he responded no, but that he was sure I'd get the same response. A meeting with the merchandise manager was arranged. Merchandise managers tend to be very tough characters, and seldom budge from the general modus operandi established by the store. At the meeting, I opened with the same question. Why such a poor representation of Polaroid's SX-70? Why no newspaper advertising? "Are you joking?" he said. "I should spend $6,000 on advertising a camera with such a limited markup? Isn't that throwing money out the window?" His attitude was clearly that I had some kind of nerve to be taking up his time with such a stupid question.

The merchandise manager was wearing penny loafers with pennies in them, a button-down shirt, khaki pants, rep tie, and a navy blue blazer. This guy had dressed straight out of a preppie handbook. It took some effort for me to keep a straight face.

Then I asked him if he had ever heard of Ray May. He said, "Of course, everybody in Denver has heard of Ray May!" At the time, Ray was star linebacker for the Denver Broncos, and the man responsible for bringing respectability to the team. After he finished with the accolades, I asked what he would think of having Ray May in his store for a Saturday, and inviting the general public to come have their picture taken with Ray May (with the Polaroid

SX-70, of course). He almost lost the pennies out of his shoes jumping to work out the details. Now my problem was to work out the logistics for the event when all this guy wanted to do was talk football. He canceled his appointments, and the man who only a few minutes before was standing with his arms folded so he could keep an eye on his watch now had all the time in the world.

I had played football with Ray in college, and since I was a Bronco fan now living in Denver, I was spending a fair amount of time with him. On the field, he was one of the most vicious tacklers ever to button a chin strap, but off the field, he was one of the nicest guys you could ever meet. Ray always had a passionate concern for the progress of young brothers, and did a lot of personal work along those lines. As a professional football player, Ray was an ideal candidate for a promotional event. It was time to ask Ray for a favor.

The store ran a full-page ad, which was the first of any size they had ever run on cameras. They stocked all of their stores with the SX-70 cameras and film. The event was a big success, with people lined up outside the store to get in. The merchandise manager was a hero. He had brought a superstar into the store, produced a visible increase in traffic and sales, and caught the eye of the store's executives.

Ray had done me an enormous favor by agreeing to appear. I gave him an SX-70 and some film. It was the first time a Polaroid marketing representative had a celebrity appear at a promotional event, and Ray May's picture graced the Polaroid quarterly publication for the next national sales meeting.

The event gave me a lot of credibility in the Denver market, and Denver Dry Goods wanted a piece of the action. They wanted to one-up the competition, so they did a two-day promotion with Ray May. Meanwhile, there was no one complaining about limited markups or the cost of advertising. Now it was "When can we do it?" The promotion didn't happen with complicated closes, it happened with planting excitement in the merchandise manager and giving him a chance to shine. A little imagination, and thinking big, got me that sale.

Getting a sports celebrity should not be a big deal for brothers and sisters, since most of these guys come from our neighborhoods. If an athlete or entertainer is from your high school or college, he or she will probably be happy to help you get a leg up. But you have to ask. Not through agents either, but by approaching the celebrity personally. Otherwise there are layers of problems you have to deal with, most of them involving huge egos. Remember—sell the sizzle, not the steak.

CLOSING THE DEAL

While working as the manager of the Hallmark Cards showcase store in Disneyland, I was afforded a great deal of freedom to roam about the park in my silly powder-blue blazer and Disney badge. I met a man who worked for a film company on weekends; his full-time job was sales manager for Flying Tiger Airlines. We were discussing business, and I was bragging about getting a territory in Beverly Hills with Hallmark Cards. I went on with how much of a soft sell it was going to be. In the most incredulous tone, my newfound friend said, "Wilson, never use the words 'soft sell' again, because there is no such thing, and it is only the mediocre businessperson who believes that there is." To make his point, he went out to his car and brought back a tape on closes by J. Douglas Edwards.

"This is yours. Use it," he said, "and I guarantee you will be a top salesman."

I started my business off with this tape of J. Douglas Edwards's closes. I've done a lot of research on what is out there on closes, and my experience has been that it comes full circle, with pretty much the same going for almost everyone. Tom Hopkins is probably the most renowned business sales trainer in America, and he uses Edwards's closes with a few twists here and there. And I am not about to reinvent the wheel.

The success of these closes depends on your remembering them, because if you don't, listening to the tape is pretty much a waste of time. Remember, you are an actor learning a script. In the business world, the heavy hitters average four to five closes to make a deal. How many closes do you know? How many do you use? The average businessperson knows two or three closes and uses only one. When do you close? It is your closing instinct that you will develop by listening. You can either close too soon or too often, but you will automatically develop the instincts. You will find your range as long as you practice. And practice, and practice, and practice.

Your success will have a lot to do with understanding the dynamics of the questions you ask, and how you respond to equivocating answers. If you remember nothing else, remember that when you ask a closing question, *shut up*. When you ask a closing question, *shut up*. The dynamics of this are absolutely incredible, because more often than not, there is silence after you ask someone a closing question. You put the pressure on them to give you an answer, and the minute you interrupt that silence, you let them off the hook. If you keep your mouth shut, one of two things will happen: the person will either go along with you and what you are presenting or give you a reason why not. As a businessperson you can cash either one. Ask a closing question—then *shut up*!

Here they are:

1. **Alternate of choice or director's close.**

   This close is when you direct the person to pick one or the other of two options. This close can be used not only in business, but in everyday life as well. "Which do you prefer, fried chicken or baked?"

   "Which do you prefer, an afternoon meeting or do you think that we can accomplish more if we met first thing tomorrow morning?"

   "Which do you prefer, purple or gold?"

   "Do you think we should use the shrink wrap on this packaging, or should we go with the less expensive cellophane?"

   Basically what you are doing is locking the other person in to a decision. You are directing them into a positive response for which you have provided the answers.

2. **Balance sheet or Ben Franklin close.**

   I resisted using this close for quite a while, probably because it sounded so hokey—but I promise you that it does work. Once you remember the principles of this close, you can vary it as you see fit. The close is used on the indecisive prospect from whom you can't get a specific reason for hesitating. Follow this script:

   "As you know, Martin, we Americans have long considered Ben Franklin one of our four wisest men. Whenever Ben found himself in a situation such as you are in today, he felt pretty much as you do about it. If it was the right thing to do, he wanted to be sure and do it. And if it was the wrong thing, he wanted to be sure to avoid it.

Isn't that about the way you feel? Here's what old Ben used to do. He'd take a plain sheet of white paper and would draw a line down the middle. Then he would write on this side [point to the left column] the word "Yes," and on this side [point to the right column] he'd write the word "No." Then, here [point to the Yes side], he would list all the reasons favoring his decision, and here [point to the No side], he would list all the reasons against it. When he was through, he simply counted the items in each column and his decision was made for him. Why don't we try it, and see what happens?"

Now you swing the paper around, put it in front of him, hand him your pen, and say, "Let's see how many reasons we can think of favoring a Yes decision to-day," and you give him all the help you can. When you get to the No side, you say, "Now let's see how many reasons you can think of against it," and then you *shut up*. You are having him write in his own handwriting all the reasons he should go along with your recommendations. Then what happens to his mind? You start him on the Yeses and his mind can't switch fast enough to think of more than three or four Nos. Then all you do is count up the columns—out loud—and when you finish, say, "Well, the answer is pretty obvious, isn't it, Martin? Should the company start moving you and your family to Seattle in December, or would January make more sense?"

3. **Summary close.**

This is an inversion of the Ben Franklin close, done orally. It is best used on the businessperson who can't give a specific reason for not going along with you. This is the Negative Yes close. You allow the client to say no, but he or she means yes. Always start this way: "Just to clarify my thinking, Norbert, what isn't quite clear to you? Is it the integrity of my proposal? Is it my personal integrity?" Then you summarize all the facets of your proposal, whatever it is for, by asking, "Is it this? Is it that?" Each time he says "No" he is saying "Yes" to you.

4. Similar situation close.

The storytelling close will probably be one of the more effective closes that you will use repeatedly in business situations. You tell the story of the success of someone doing exactly what you told them to do, or how someone didn't listen to your advice and was sorry for it. Telling stories builds rapport. And if you have a shortage of stories, may I suggest you read *Talk That Talk*, which is an anthology of African American storytelling, collected by Arthur Huff Fauset. The story "No Tracks Coming Back" goes like this: You know, Brer Rabbit was said to be the wisest animal in the forest. So Brer Rabbit was walkin' along one day when Brer Fox came along. "Say, Brer Rabbit," Brer Fox says, "ain't you goin' to de big meetin'? Everybody goin'." "Xat so," says Brer Rabbit, "sure I'm goin'." So Brer Fox went off an' Brer Rabbit he take a look around. Pretty soon he sees hundreds o' footprints an' "Mmm," says Brer Rabbit. "All dem tracks goin' dat way, an' not a single one comin' dis way. Dat ain't no place fo' me."

Your own imagination will tell you how you can use this story.

5. Call-back close.

In business, there is no such thing as a good call-back. About the only thing you can do to save a call-back situation is to start off by saying, "I am very sorry, but the last time I was here there was something

I forgot to tell you, and I think it is important." Then you tell the client something new (anything new). As soon as you have told him something new, go on with "Malcolm, let me just review briefly the things we talked about last time." Now give him the entire presentation all over again, using "As you remember," "You will recall," "You agreed that," etc., and then go into a normal closing sequence.

6. **Sharp-angle close.**

Close at the buying signals. When someone asks you if your product does this or that, it is very easy to say yes it does this, or yes it comes in that color. So if someone says, "Can it do this?" you sharp angle them by saying, "Do you want it if it does?" If they say "Yes," you have a commitment that this customer will buy upon proof that it does this or that. If you don't sharp angle the customer, but simply answer "Yes," all you have done is answer a question. Don't ever waste the opportunity to get a commitment, be it for your product, proposal, or plan.

7. **I'll-think-it-over close.**

This is the most often used objection. Basically people don't want to make a commitment, so they will say, "I'll think it over and get back to you." The only problem with that is that they never do. At least almost never. If you let it go at that, there is really nothing tangible or specific to put your teeth into. What you are after is a specific objection. You can handle a specific objection. So when someone says, "I'll think it over," you will be saying to yourself, *face*, because you will be slammin' and jammin'.

The businessperson is not the kind to make a snap

judgment, and wants to think it over. You say, "That's fine, Paul. Obviously you wouldn't take time to think it over unless you were really interested, would you?" (Let him say yes.) "I am sure that you are not telling me that just to get rid of me, so may I assume that you will give it very careful consideration?"

Now Paul thinks you're letting him go and will undoubtedly say, "Yes, I'll give it very careful consideration." Then you hit him with the face job: "Just to clarify my thinking, Paul, what phase of this program is it that you want to think over? Is it the integrity of Real McCoy Oil?" You must get in the first "is it" without stopping, or he will say he wants to think over the whole thing. You go on with all the positive things about your program—is it the shipping, is it my integrity, is it the color—until he grabs on to something. He could say something like "It's the shipping." At which time you have something tangible to deal with. "So if it were not for the shipping, you would accept my recommendation?" If he says "Yes" and you can handle that objection, then you will be successful in that transaction.

8. **Wilson's close number one: the Columbo close.**

Named after the TV series. The sale seems to be dead. You start packing up like you are leaving. You have the resigned look of having given up. In a befuddled tone you ask, "Marian, obviously I make my living this way, and I have a few other accounts who are in a similar situation as yourself. I need a favor from you—would you give me some ideas about how to sell our new camera to my next account?" When she gives you the ideas, you say, "Now, why didn't I think of that? What else?" You let her sell herself, and allow your normal closing sequence to go to work afterward.

9. **Wilson's close number two: the M.T. Hammer close (too legit to quit).**

This close is named after my old buddy Michael Thompson: you don't leave the premises until you ask at least five times. Even if you don't get the results, you must ask for the order at least five times, in five different ways. Follow these examples:

MR. LOVE: Michael, are you going to pay for your health club membership with a credit card or with a check? (close 1)

MICHAEL: Thank you, Mr. Love, but I don't think that I am ready to be a member in a health club at this time.

MR. LOVE: What are your reservations about joining now?

MICHAEL: My wife and I want to work out together, and we have two small children.

MR. LOVE: If I understand you correctly, you need someone to watch the children while you and your wife work out.

MICHAEL: Exactly!

MR. LOVE: You will be happy to know that we have a baby-sitting service on the premises. I apologize for not showing you the baby-sitting facility earlier. Will you be putting this membership in any other names besides you and your wife? (close 2)

MICHAEL: No.

MR. LOVE: Good, what is your correct mailing address?

MICHAEL: Whoa . . . wait a minute. I didn't say that I was going to buy a membership just yet.

MR. LOVE: Michael, you want to get in shape, right?

MICHAEL: Right!

MR. LOVE: And your wife wants to get rid of a couple of pounds, right?

MICHAEL: Right!

MR. LOVE: And this is a convenient location for you, is it not?

MICHAEL: Yes.

MR. LOVE: Then let's get you started, as they say in those commercials . . . let's just do it now. Do you and your wife play racquetball?

MICHAEL: No, but we have been thinking about learning.

MR. LOVE: Fantastic, we have a pro on the premises that gives private and group lessons. It's only $4 more per month, should I include that on your membership? (close 3)

MICHAEL: Sounds great, but I need to think about it, and I'll get back to you.

MR. LOVE: That's fine, Michael. Just to clarify my thinking . . . (See close #7, I'll think it over.) (close 4)

MICHAEL: I guess the bottom line is that $300 is a little much to be giving up all at once.

MR. LOVE: So if it wasn't for the large investment up front, you would join tonight?

MICHAEL: You betcha.

MR. LOVE: Michael, I understand exactly how you feel, and I also know that you and your wife want to get in shape. With our wonderful facilities you are going to feel right at home. We have a payment plan that is designed for the working couple. You pay only $15 a month, and we will make it convenient for you so it's taken out of your checking account automatically. Your total start-up tonight is only $30. What is the correct spelling of your wife's first name? (close 5)

10. **Feel, felt, found close.**

    This is one of your epic closes because it sounds good and it works. "Othello, I know exactly how you *feel*. I work with an account who *felt* the same way, and he *found* once he adopted this method of writing memos, he never went back to his original."

11. **Puppy dog close.**

If you want to sell a puppy dog, you let someone take it home. And the puppy pretty much sells itself. So consider that when you want someone to buy something that you know will work for them.

EXCUSES

Closes only facilitate your argument for that person to whom you are selling: If you have more closes than the customer has excuses, it's virtually a slam dunk. If a guy has three excuses and you have two closes, you lose. But if you have five closes and he has three excuses, it's two points for sure. The problem is that most businesspeople know three closes or less and tend to use only one, which I've found to be the biggest reason most businesspeople shun accounts that won't buy from them on the first close. Ninety percent of the salespeople that you meet will be "order takers." When someone makes an excuse not to buy, they smile and leave.

My grandaddy told this story about excuses. He had a neighbor who used to borrow his lawnmower, but every time Grandaddy needed to cut his own lawn, he had to go over to his neighbor's house to borrow his own lawnmower. Finally, Grandaddy had enough, and the next time his neighbor asked to borrow the lawnmower Grandaddy said, "I can't loan it to you anymore." The neighbor asked, "Why?" Grandaddy said, "Because I just bought my son Illinois a new saxophone." His neighbor exclaimed, "Gilbert, what the hell does your buying your son a saxophone have to do with my borrowing your lawnmower?" Grandaddy replied, "Well, Rufus, it has nothing to do with it—but one excuse is just as good as another!" When it's all said and done, it's the scoreboard, baby!

GETTING PAST GATEKEEPERS

To further maneuver your way through the corporation, you have to know how to crash gates and be heard.

No executive really has time to see you. This fact is told to you by executive secretaries over and over again. Many secretaries earn their stripes by keeping people at bay. Many will tell you that they flat out run the business, which is not true. The toughest part of any business arrangement is not talking to the decision makers of the company, as you might assume. It is getting past the various lines of defense they have constructed around themselves.

Receptionists are generally the first line, and they are the easiest to get by. They try hard to stop you, but they are by the nature of their position restricted in the number of questions that they can ask you. So they say something like "Coors Beer. May I direct your call?"

"Yes, I would like to speak to Haven Moses in Marketing. Is he available?"

"He's in a meeting. May I take a message for him?" Don't let the receptionist stop you even if he is in a meeting. Proceed with "Put me through to his secretary please. He is expecting my call." Your objective is to get past this first line of defense.

Your voice plays a big part in clearing this hurdle. The tone must suggest that you were supposed to call and that this person has no business stopping you. Your voice should be matter-of-fact, but authoritative. If the receptionist detects any weakness in your voice, you will become another notch in the Brownie point scoresheet of intruders who have been stopped at the gates. Receptionists have been programmed to be cautious and protective in directing calls, but they also know that if they stop the wrong call it could mean their jobs. The second you detect the receptionist feeling out the call, attack. A firm "*Would you put me through to Mr. Haven Moses, please*" will generally do the trick. At the very least she will pass you through to the second line of defense and let the personal secretary make the fateful decision.

The second line of defense is not quite that easy. You're talking to the personal secretary now, and his or her job is to keep you away for real. This secretary is the last line of defense and is not prone to sweet talk. In many cases, these secretaries believe that they should be running the show. The fact is many of them could. Many of them will tell you to mail them something and they will get back to you. But don't bite. Once you do that, you have hell to pay getting past them.

Again, mind-set is everything. The words are critical and so is the emotion. The slightest suggestion of weakness and you are dog meat. They eat up a couple dozen callers a day, and they relish taking you apart. Some of them will tear your head off just to keep in shape. However, the bottom line is that they don't make the decisions, they don't sign any paychecks, and if something goes wrong for bosses, secretaries will bury their heads in their PCs as if they didn't know that anything was wrong at all.

The ones that are really good take lunch at the same time almost every day. Top executive secretaries are highly organized and leave and arrive like clockwork. They always have someone taking their place when they are gone. So there are always ways to get past them if you find one who is particularly difficult to deal with.

Generally the secretary will ask you what your call is regarding. You answer with "My name is _____ and I am with _____. Is Haven available?" Don't use Mr. or the last name when you ask for the decision maker. You have actually asked a question. Is he there? So you might get the response "Yes, he is. May I tell him what this is about?" This is a critical point, because it's the secretary's best move to stop you, and if you give the wrong answer, you're dead in the water. Tell the secretary you are following up on some correspondence with Haven, and you are going to be in Denver in two weeks, and you just want to poke your head in to say hello. "Would you put me through to him please?" Now wait for the response. You have made the secretary think. You have also given him or her a decision to make. The secretary could put you through or could start telling you about the boss's schedule. If the secretary is bold enough to give the schedule to you, then find out when the boss will be in town. The words are not nearly as important as the attitude. If you are bold and forthright, you will almost always get through.

If you do not go through a switchboard, then ask the secretary for his/her name. Use it each time you call. Introduce yourself: give your name clearly and spell it, if necessary. Treat the secretary with dignity and respect. State the nature of your call or remind the secretary of your last contact, if there was one. If you have been referred, explain that a mutual acquaintance had suggested getting together (remember you are only seeking information and advice, not asking for a job). If the secretary says, "We're not hiring," explain again that you are not looking for a job, only advice, and that the referral was supplied by a mutual friend. If you are following up on a letter and the secretary says, "Oh, Mr./Ms. so and so, your letter has been sent to the Personnel Department," determine whether it was sent at the boss's direction. If so, get the name and number of the personnel executive. If it was not sent at the boss's direction, send another letter to the boss to make contact, but first inform the secretary of your intention so the letter will be put through. If a letter that you wrote after missing each other several times by phone was not received or remembered, send another and follow up with a phone call.

State, "I'll call you again" whenever you have not established contact with the boss and after asking if there is a best time for your return call. Avoid saying, "Have him or her call me please." Maintain control of the situation by calling again yourself.

If you have had previous contact, leave a message for the boss to return your call. However, if you do not hear from the boss, call back. Leave a message when it is not necessary to talk directly with the boss. Thank the secretary for the assistance. Arrange or confirm an appointment directly with the secretary.

The decision-maker himself or herself may be surprised when you get through, and some of them will put on an air of invincibility. Like, how did you get through, and what do you want? My approach has always been to come right to the point as soon as possible. Don't dance; go right for the jugular. "Haven, I am going to be in Denver in two weeks on business, and your secretary said that you would be in town. Would it be better to poke my head in Tuesday morning or is there another time better for you that week?" You have now created a situation in which anything short of the boss telling you to get lost, which he or she will be reluctant to do if you're from a credible organization (the boss has not had time to calculate the pros and cons), is a win. Nothing wrong with your poking your head in, is there? It doesn't have to take up a whole lot of time, does it? Not much to put up with to make the company look good to a major charitable organization or supplier, is it? Now you confirm the date and you immediately send out a letter confirming the appointment. You make as many appointments as you can in a particular city.

THE ART OF LISTENING

Of all the skills that you perfect, none is more important than listening. If you perfect this skill, not only will you do well as a businessperson, you will do well in life. Many salespeople and businesspeople alike are known as talkers, and their image is certainly one of having the gift of gab. The truth is that the superior individual in the business community is not the one with the continuous dialogue, but rather the one who listens.

The thirteen steps listed below will be your guide to developing your power listening skills. You will want to read and reread them until the steps become a part of the way that you do business. This will be one time that thirteen will mean good luck.

THIRTEEN STEPS TO POWER LISTENING

1. *Limit your own talking.* You can't talk and listen at the same time. That is a fact. Learn how to keep your presentation brief.
2. *Think like the other person.* Their problems and needs are important and you'll understand and retain them better if you can focus on their point of view.
3. *Ask questions.* If you don't understand some-

thing or feel you may have missed a point, clear it up now before it comes back to bite you in the butt later.

4. *Don't interrupt.* A pause—even a long pause—doesn't always mean the other person has finished.

5. *Concentrate.* Focus your mind on what's being said. Practice shutting out distractions.

6. *Take notes.* This will help you remember important points. But be selective. Trying to jot down everything can result in being left far behind in retaining relevant details, and it can be distracting, giving the impression that you are preparing a rebuttal.

7. *Listen for ideas, not just words.* You want to get the whole picture, not jut isolated bits and pieces. You want to know where the speaker is coming from.

8. *Interject.* An occasional "yes" or "I see" shows the speaker you're still with them—but don't overdo it.

9. *Turn off your own thoughts.* This is the toughest part of listening, but personal fears, worries, problems not connected with your business contact, form a kind of "static" in your own brain that can blank out the customer's message.

10. *Prepare in advance.* Remarks and questions prepared in advance free your mind for listening.

11. *React to ideas, not words.* Don't allow irritation at things others may say, or at their manner, to distract you. It doesn't matter if you like or agree with where they are coming from, you just need to find out what their position is.

12. *Don't jump to conclusions.* Avoid making un-

warranted assumptions about what the person is going to say, or mentally trying to complete sentences for them. Nothing is more annoying than being cut off in midsentence. Even if you are right, it is still annoying.

13. *Listen for the undertones.* You can learn a great deal about people from the way they say things and the way they react to the things you say. How their day is going can be heard in someone's voice.

5

Setting and Achieving Goals

*For every disciplined effort
there is a multiple reward.*
—JIM ROBN

Having goals is of paramount importance in life. Without goals you just wander aimlessly, paying rent and trying to figure out what you want to be when you grow up. Most people make better plans for a party than they do for life. To excel in the business world, you need to have not only goals, but an action plan to reach those goals. You not only need to write your goals down on a piece of paper, but you need to be specific about them and they need to be achievable. Once you have completed that, you need to take action. Sound pretty simple? That's because it is.

Most people don't put their goals in writing. And most people do not commit to their goals. The worst thing you can do is put down goals that you know are not achievable. At a goal-setting seminar I heard the following story, which describes setting unrealistic goals.

SET REALISTIC GOALS

There was this guy who was a bag man for the Mafia, and one day he decided that his goal was to keep the money, not deliver it to the proper people. He buried the bag money near a tree in his backyard. What was unique about this bag man was that he was a deaf mute. But, none-theless, he had set a goal and he was sticking to it. Within hours of the time he was supposed to deliver the money, the mafia had sent two very large and very mean hit men to the door of this deaf mute to recover the money. One man was six-foot-five and weighed about three hundred pounds. He had a wide scar that went across his face from the top of his forehead to the bottom of his chin. I'm talking about a mean-looking dude. His partner was not nearly as impos-ing, but he knew sign language.

They busted the door down and the deaf mute was just sitting calmly in his chair. The interpreter signed to the mute to hand over the money. The mute signed back say-ing that he didn't have the money. The interpreter signed back saying that they were not joking, and if he didn't come up with the money, his partner Tiny was going to shoot him. The mute thought to himself, No—I set a goal and I am going to stick with it. He signed back, saying, "I don't have the money." Tiny said, "What did he say?" His partner said, "He doesn't have it."

Tiny pulled out his .44 Magnum and put it to the mute's head. The interpreter signed again, saying, "If you don't tell us where the money is, Tiny is going to blow your brains out, and we are not joking." Finally, the mute figured that his goal was unrealistic, so he signed back to the interpreter that the money was in the backyard, near the tree. Tiny, waving the Magnum nervously at the mute's head, asked again, "What did he say?" The interpreter looked up at Tiny and said, "He says you don't have the guts to pull that trigger."

The Lesson: Be realistic about your goals!

DEVELOP A BURNING DESIRE

It's very important to have achievable goals. The goals should be challenging and they should provide direction to your efforts. How else do you measure your progress? But you also need to have a burning desire to reach your goals. If you ask most people about their number one goal, you'll find that money heads the list. It's not an unrealistic goal, but the question must be, what do you want to do with the money? I suggest you arrange in your mind exactly what you will do with the money that you earn. This way your vague goal (to earn money) becomes a realistic, achievable one, with a set of preordained steps you can take to achieve it.

If you want to buy a home or a car, or even if you just want to take a nice vacation, be specific about your goals and write them down that way. Every time you look at them, they become more real, and help generate the determination and effort to achieve them. Then develop a realistic, workable plan. (Save a certain amount each month, for example.)

If your goal is to have your own company, determine how you can make that happen. Learn the business, do your research, acquire the capital you need before you hang your shingle outside the door. Remember, the key to goal attainment is to write it down, be specific, and devise a plan of attack.

PRACTICE TIME MANAGEMENT

To excel in the business world and to reach the goals you set for yourself, you have to be an effective and self-disciplined manager of time. The great thing about time is that everyone has the same amount. It doesn't matter how much money you have, where you live, or what your background is. We all get twenty-four hours a day, which no one can steal from us. There are seminars, books, and endless articles on time management, so if you need help, a trip to the library or bookstore should get you started. Otherwise, there are a few pointers below.

Among the aimless, unsuccessful, or worthless, you often hear talk about "killing time." The brothers or sisters who are always "killing time" are really killing their chances in life, while those who are destined to succeed are those who make every minute count.

After twenty years in corporate America, I am convinced that the following are the most common traps for sabotaging your goals.

TEN WAYS TO SABOTAGE YOUR GOALS:

1. *The unplanned day.* There's a saying that "the person who doesn't know where he is headed usually winds up someplace else." It's a great temptation just to get started and plan the day as you go along by "playing it by ear." This is like a ship that leaves shore without charting a course. The ship will either drift off with the winds or end up shipwrecked.

    At the end of each day, take a few minutes to outline what you hope to accomplish the next day.

How many hours of actual work do you plan to shoot for? Be specific about what your first action of the day is going to be. It has been my experience that it is best to tackle first the most difficult item on your list of things to do. Once the most unpleasant item is out of the way, you'll get a psychological lift because you will realize that only a few minutes into the day you've done the toughest thing you had to do. From there on, it's a piece of cake.

Unplanned days mean unplanned weeks, months, and years. The key to effective planning is to do it in writing. *Remember, a mental note is not worth the paper it's written on.*

2. *The unused telephone.* The telephone is the second most important business tool. (The first, of course, is your mind.) In addition to making generous use of the telephone for scheduling, it is important to use it in lieu of personal contact in those situations where it is appropriate.

   The phone is particularly effective when the need is to prioritize your business contacts in relation to the volume of business they generate. Establishing the optimum ratio between personal contacts and phone contacts in any given business situation is something that can be done only on the basis of experience. But don't downgrade the telephone because of habit, custom, or prejudice. It can spell the difference between success and failure.

   Often a quick phone call instead of popping your head in a colleague's door will keep business brief and to the point.

3. *Unqualified business prospects.* Time is far too

precious to squander on a business prospect list that hasn't been screened, analyzed, researched, evaluated, updated, checked, and double-checked. Ask yourself the following questions:

- Does the list of business contacts that I have need to be prequalified with advance phone calls?
- Why am I working from this particular list of contacts?
- Are there business prospect sources that may have been overlooked?
- When was the last time these contacts were called on?

Before calling on any particular company, ask, Is this company large enough so that if we do business it will be big enough to give me an adequate return on my time invested? Above all, ask, Is this company on my list just because I always receive a warm and friendly reception there, even though we never do any business? If the answer to this question is yes, cross that company off your list immediately, or seek another line of work.

4. *The haphazard travel schedule.* In their eagerness to get away from the office, many businesspeople forget that the time they spend traveling in the air is sometimes wasted, whereas time invested in planning, phoning, and rescheduling, in order to maximize the ratio of face-to-face time to travel time, is time well spent. That applies to trips to the other side of town as well as cross-country journeys.

Schedule your business meetings to maximize your time so that when you park your car, you are in the vicinity to make at least two or three calls. With the advent of car phones, you can confirm your appointments while driving. If you have planned your calls on one side of town and your first appointment is not ready, a simple phone call will set up the next one. The problem is that some people confuse activity with achievement. Driving from one appointment to another helter-skelter creates an illusion of working hard, when usually it adds up to little more than spinning your wheels.

5. *The long lunch*. If time is money, it is then irresponsible to let lunchtime drift into the late afternoon. When I first started in corporate America, there were very few brothers and sisters in the business. We were so happy to see one another that a few of us decided to meet for lunch to discuss our presence in the work force. The only problem is that the lunch lasted until 3 P.M., and generally we ended up at someone's home, wasting the whole day.

My suggestion is that you spend that hour or so at the gym, or with a client. Even with a client, it is prudent to keep an eye on the clock. Not only does the customer have his own work to get back to, but he will respect you more if you establish a businesslike atmosphere by indicating, after an appropriate time, that you have other appointments.

6. *The lunchtime drink*. Don't do it, ever. Don't drink, don't light up a doobie, don't take a pill or a snort. The easiest way to lose your edge is to take a drink or drug. Generally, one drink leads

to another, which then increases the appetite. One way or another, the result is less business.

7. *The short day.* Often the difference between the star and the mediocre businessperson is the amount of time each spends at work. One starts late and ends early, while the other starts early and remains until well after 5 P.M. It's easy to rationalize the late start and the early stop. My philosophy has always been the light-coffee syndrome. I am the first one in the office, so I make the coffee. And since I'm the last one to leave, I also turn off the lights.

My first job out of college was with Hallmark Cards. Hallmark gave me the opportunity to work on the retail end as a store manager in their showcase store on Main Street in Disneyland. My responsibilities as store manager included merchandising, hiring, ordering product, and public relations. At that time, in 1972, Disneyworld had not yet opened for business; we were the only show.

My boss became my mentor, and the best advice he gave me was in response to the question, "How do I become the best marketing representative in the country?" "Wilson," he said, "Start early and when you're ready to go home, make one more call." "Is that it?" I said. "That's it," he replied. If you manage one more call each day, your business will increase. Don't cheat yourself out of sales by telling yourself that five o'clock isn't the best time of day to make a call.

8. *The Friday afternoon syndrome.* A lot of people fudge by leaving the office early on Friday afternoon. But many don't. That business contact that

you have been trying to reach all week may be in the second category. So don't finesse yourself out of doing business by jumping to an unwarranted conclusion.

If for some reason you really are unable to chalk up face-to-face time late on Friday afternoon, at least use the time constructively by doing paperwork and planning for the week to come. I guarantee that you will enjoy your weekend if you do.

9. *Shooting the bull.* This is an occupational hazard in business, and it's not hard to understand why. The businessperson is traditionally a people person, with a natural ability to interact with people. Swapping stories and telling jokes with colleagues, or discussing sports with friendly customers, seems to be the norm.

Unfortunately, those pleasant interludes don't move you any closer to your goals. Socializing has its place, but when those friendly coffee breaks are running into that third cup of coffee, find some way to gently extricate yourself and you'll find that your business will benefit.

10. *Inefficient paperwork and other office obstacles.* Obsession with paperwork isn't the key to doing business—quite the contrary. The things to avoid are getting bogged down with unnecessary paperwork and spending time in the office that should be spent across the desk from a business contact (for instance, writing a letter to a client when a phone call would be quicker and more effective). In other words, paperwork can be a diversionary device, a way of making yourself think you're working.

Of course, the necessary paperwork must be done, and should be done promptly. Just keep paperwork to a minimum and keep it current.

Remember that your desk is not a place for trophies, awards, food, clothing, and non-job sundries. If these things are on your desk, the stack becomes a distraction. You have a difficult time completing projects because you have all these other things to think about. So have only what you are working on in front of you.

Keep your objectives in mind, and ask yourself over and over again, Is what I am doing right now contributing directly to reaching my goals? If not, why am I doing it?

Self-worth cannot be verified by others.
You are worthy because you say it is so. If you depend
on others for your value,
it is other-worth.
—Dr. Wayne Dyer

TIPS FROM THE PROS

BERNARD KINSEY, CONSULTANT

What kind of advice would you give for goal setting and achievement?

I think first of all you really need to look at a career, secondly look at your life plan. I developed a life plan fifteen to twenty years ago. I've been married almost thirty years, and my wife and I, we work toward our life goals first and then the career goals help fund them. But career is not the primary and only motivator. When you think about it, when you have kids, what are you going to do with your kids, where are they going to go to college? What kinds of vacations, hobbies and educational objectives are you going to pursue as an individual? Five years out of a black college I went and got an MBA, because back in the seventies MBAs were hot tickets. They are still hot tickets up to a point, but they are not as hot as they once were because everybody has one. Doesn't mean that you shouldn't go for one; it just means that you should understand that there're a lot more people got the same ticket to get in the same event. But in terms of goal setting, the thing that I have always done is to set my standards high. If you don't set your standards high, you're probably going to miss your objectives. And when I say set your standards high, I was working with the LA Chief of Police Willie Williams, and I've always said look two levels higher than where you are. You look at two levels above where you are and you can begin to model your behavior behind and around people who are successful. Have at least seven goals. Have one for your spiritual self . . . personal self . . . family . . . Have one for being a mother or father . . . Have one for your job . . . Have one for the community. And have a life plan which encompasses the whole.

What are some of the mistakes African Americans make in corporate America?

I think the biggest mistake is to think that we are only 10 percent of the market—and I have heard this so many times—and not believe that the company belongs to us, too. I did not have that attitude when I worked for Humble Oil and I did not have that attitude when I worked for Xerox. I said this is my company, too, and I have a right to make recommendations and comments about how the company should run and do business. And also in terms of getting the kind of leadership ability that will make people begin to listen to Bernard Kinsey. A lot of people have a lot of strong ideas, but they don't have the kind of attributes and positive characteristics that anybody will follow. My definition for leadership is simply if you look behind you and somebody is following then you are a leader, and if nobody's behind you then you are not a leader. You have to find out what the things are that you are displaying that will cause people to follow you.

RHONDA WINDHAM, PUBLIC RELATIONS AND
PROMOTIONS, LA LAKERS

What kind of advice would you give for goal setting and achievement?
All goals are attainable. Don't expect people to congratulate you when you are successful. You must find self-worth and gratification within.

JOHN KELLY, PRESIDENT/CEO, ENTERPRISE
NATIONAL BANK

What kind of advice would you give for goal setting and achievement?
Over the years, I've found the most successful way to monitor my career success has been to establish a five-year plan. Strategically identify where you want to be in your career in five-year intervals. Start from your first job, and continue to your present position and beyond. Every five years, reassess your accomplishments as compared to goals established, and revise the five-year plan. This process helped me to reach the highest levels I wanted to achieve in banking, and to do so within my time and not the bank's.
What are some of the mistakes African Americans make in corporate America?

African Americans in corporate America tend to believe they have made it and, therefore, racism, bias, and ignorance do not exist. When you enter the corporate world, it is more likely that you will be judged by higher standards and paid on a lower pay scale than your white counterparts. The most successful African Americans in the banking industry used the sponsor approach to moving up the ladder. Pick your friends, and identify and hold your mentor. Keep a low profile and limit your socializing; after all, this is a job, not an after hours' club. Don't buy into the myth that white management views you as equal. While the company may be socially minded, the leadership is only human. Do your job and do it well. Remember that a professional attitude is everything to an African American in corporate America. Above all, don't play where you work!

PAT WATTS, SOUTHERN CALIFORNIA EDISON

What kind of advice would you give for goal setting and achievement?

Focus on your goal, develop a strategy and a timetable to achieve the goal. Set realistic goals and timetables and celebrate each success. Reevaluate your goals periodically to make sure you are in sync with the current times.

What are some of the mistakes African Americans make in corporate America?

Accepting defeat, not realizing that they are being set up for failure. Not showing consistent determination to achieve their personal goals. Not seeking mentorships. Not believing in themselves. Not pursuing restitution for unjust or unfair evaluation on their performance, through processes established within the organization. Not being willing to go all the way to the legal system if a pattern of inequality or denial of opportunity for advancement continues to be evident. (In particular when less qualified individuals continue to advance.)

WILLIAM BURTIES, ASSISTANT VICE PRESIDENT,
UNION BANK

What kind of advice would you give for goal setting and achievement?

My advice would be to set daily, monthly, and yearly goals. To accomplish the goals you must be persistent and determined. Don't allow criticism or praise to interfere with your achieving your goals.

What are some of the mistakes African Americans make in corporate America?

The fine balance between being too aggressive and being too passive seems to be the dilemma for all of us. Without a mentor to guide us, I think it will always be difficult to fit in to white corporate America.

GAIL BLAKE SMITH, PACIFIC BELL

What are some of the mistakes African Americans make in corporate America?

A lot of companies believe in higher education and they help subsidize that. Pacific Bell will pay 100 percent for you to go to any college you want to on a part-time basis as long as you maintain a C average. African Americans traditionally have not taken advantage of this. Secondly, we don't take advantage of the investments with the company, like savings bonds, 401 Ks, stock options. Whatever is available, I encourage everyone to take full advantage, because it's free money and you are stupid if you don't seize the opportunity. Be proactive and reactive.

MICHAEL THOMPSON, POLAROID CORPORATION

What are some of the mistakes African Americans make in corporate America?

Boy, I could tell you the first mistake that I made. And that was not being politically astute enough. I say that because coming out of our culture, we frequently look upon politics or the concept of being political as distasteful. The fact is, as a group of people, we are being very dishonest when we make that kind of a statement. The fact is, we are very political, in our families, schools, churches, fraternities, sororities. But when we come to corporations that involve white people, we want to make this a racial thing. And it's really not.

Politics comes from the same root as the French word *polite*. It's just a matter of being sensitive and caring about other people. Including yourself. I don't think this has to be a value statement. I think you can be political and still stay within the boundaries of your values.

I think the next mistake, and it's kind of akin to the first one, is that frequently we've been too focused on trying to establish mentors. And we keep finding that mentors have not been as easily available to us, and we've used that as a reason for not moving forward. I have to say that as black people, we really can't afford to concentrate so much energy on the involvement of mentors. We should be focusing on building alliances and relationships up and down and across the board, both vertically and horizontally. It's good to have a mentor, if somebody wants to assume that role. The drawback is, if you have a mentor and you identify with that mentor and something happens to him or her, you're basically down the tubes. But when you build alliances and you build across the board, you're not dependent on any one individual. You just have good solid relationships, and out of that can come the information, the support, and a lot of the other things that are needed to move up.

The third mistake we make is that frequently we go into corporations and we cease to be ourselves as African American men and women. Which is unfortunate because, if you think about who and what we are all about, we're probably some of the most creative people in the world. When we take this aspect of our personality, and we hide it, we limit a major part of our potential contribution as African American people. I think you can be very openly African American in the way you operate and not be intimidating or offensive. I'm not talking about using the street vernacular, splitting verbs, or being insulting, which often tends to get confused with "black identity" in the inner city. I think that you can still be very black, very African American, and maintain your credibility and the respect of the majority of the community. It's also important in terms of good mental health. I think all that is necessary is to maintain a balance if you want to be successful.

PART III

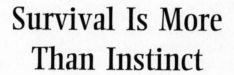

Survival Is More Than Instinct

Nothing in the world can take the place of persistence. Talent will not; nothing is more common than unsuccessful men with talent. Genius will not; unrewarded genius is almost a proverb. Education will not; the world is full of educated derelicts. Persistence and determination alone are omnipotent.

—CALVIN COOLIDGE

6

Corporate Culture

*Be aware of no one more than yourself; we carry our
worst enemies within us.*
—CHARLES SPURGEON

Corporate America has two cultures all its own. One you
see and one you don't. The culture reminds me of my time
in the military, which the Corporate Culture is built on.
You have to be very careful how you interact in business,
because corporate America is not like war, it *is* war.

After I had completed basic training in California, the
U.S. Army sent me to Fort Bragg, North Carolina, OJT
(on the job training) to be a part of the 13th PsyOps (Psychological Operations). One of my many duties as an off-
set press operator was to print propaganda leaflets that
the Army dropped from airplanes in various parts of Vietnam. You couldn't read the printed material because it
was all in Vietnamese. But the photographs appeared to
be of high-profile Vietnamese officials, partying on the
beach. The print shop had two 30-foot web presses, and
they ran day and night printing these leaflets.

My experience in printing and a secret clearance allowed me access to everything that went on in our print

shop. We printed everything from formal stationery for the John F. Kennedy Center, to training manuals for the Special Forces.

There were frequent occasions when two of us would be called from the Army print shop to take a jeep to the Green Berets and Special Forces compound. We would take Polaroid snaps of visiting dignitaries, politicians, and businessmen sitting in open-air bleachers waiting for instructions from the host. The Green Berets would take these men on a tour of the compound, showing off their technical know-how and sophisticated weaponry. At the end of the show, the all-male group would be escorted back to the bleachers. They were then addressed by one of the full-bird (colonel) Green Berets. While the colonel was talking, a helicopter would hover about the bleachers and drop leaflets over the heads of the visitors. These men in suits were like little kids when they saw those leaflets with their photographs on them. It was like a game to them.

Now everybody has some game in him; it's just the nature of man. And corporate America has plenty of game for you. It's part of the subculture and has very little to do with your being black. That's the tricky part, because the same little games are played on white men more than they are played on brothers and sisters. Once you recognize the games, you are able to deal with them more intelligently, and less emotionally. Because of their abundance, you could write several books just about the mind games.

Consider for a minute a white man coming to your neighborhood basketball court to shoot a little hoop. Unless he is escorted by a brother that is down in that neighborhood, chances are he won't play at all. Suppose he does play and he's got a really good game. The neighborhood has some rules, and one of them is if you're an outsider, you don't put anything in that hoop. If you're white, you will get fouled for even thinking about bringing anything to the hole. In Compton, California, brothers would not care if it were Jerry West in his prime. You bring that basketball inside and you had best be paid up on your medical insurance. Nothing personal. The dynamics are such that a white man's presence changes the chemistry of everyone's play.

If you're unlucky enough to be guarding a white cat that can really play and he is burying jumpers, your teammates will be on your case like it's the seventh game of the NBA finals. I've had the experience of guarding a white guy who had played college basketball, and he cleaned my clock. And I did everything including carve my name on his arms and chest with my nails. To no avail, I might add.

Corporate America views its business domain the same way—nothing personal, it's just the way it is. So it doesn't really matter who you are. The game is tough. Obviously, being a brother or sister on the white man's turf makes it tougher. Like hoop, corporate America has many nuances that are part of the game. The following list is all you need to know. Let's call it . . .

THE DIRTY DOZEN

1. *Keeping secrets.* As number-one marketing manager in the country for Polaroid Corporation, you would think that I avoided unnecessary grief. My immediate supervisor had other ideas and he seemed to have it in for me. He tried everything in his arsenal to force me to resign. Finally, he got his supervisor to join him on beating me up. Two managers playing mind games is no fun. My super-

visor's boss just happened to be a brother but he still bought into the game.

At one of the company's national meetings, I went up to this brother and requested a minute of his time. I asked if he approached our initial meeting with an open mind, or had he formed an opinion before he arrived to work with me? My belief was that if he had prejudged my performance, then he should come back to visit me with an open mind. He found the request to be reasonable and did come back.

After working with me for half a day, he told me that he had seen enough. We stopped and had lunch and he apologized to me. As a matter of fact, he felt so badly about his part in the game my supervisor was playing that the brother formulated a plan whereby I could move back to Los Angeles and be promoted all in the same move. All I had to do was listen to him. He was true to his word; in less than a week, he arranged for one of the vice presidents to work with me with the understanding that I would be promoted as per his approval. My immediate boss knew that the VP was coming to town, but what he didn't know was that he was coming specifically to be with me.

At the same time, I was being heavily recruited by another blue chip company. I had initially gone to the interview for my own ego and to see what I was worth. I asked for a ridiculous sum of money, at least in my mind. To my surprise, the blue-chip company said yes to everything that I asked for, and the only thing left in the hiring process was a meeting with one of the vice presidents. It was a cursory interview because the man I would work for wanted me on his team.

Wouldn't you know it, the very same day that I was supposed to meet with the blue-chip VP was the day that the vice president from my company was going to work with me. So I called the recruiter and told him that I could not interview with the blue-chip company, and I was no longer interested in the job. I thought the recruiter had been pretty fair with me so I explained that the VP from my company was coming to town on the same day and I was up for a promotion. The recruiter was furious because he saw his giant commission check going out the window and a lot of time wasted.

That night I got a call from the brother in Los Angeles who was setting the whole thing up. His first words were "Wilson, didn't I tell you not to tell *anyone* about the meeting with the vice president?" I defended myself because I was sure that I had not told anyone. And in my mind I had not. While I was defending myself, the brother blurted out, "You told the recruiter everything that I told you." I was stunned. He followed up with "If I tell you something and say don't tell anyone, that means don't even tell your mama!" What a tough lesson about opening your big mouth. Not only did I screw myself pretty royally, but I also compromised my newfound mentor. The end result was I did not get the job in Los Angeles.

Keeping secrets also eliminates gossip, which is another part of the subculture to avoid. You want to be in on the grapevine, but to earn that privilege, you've got to let those in the know trust your discretion and your ability to keep a secret.

The Lesson: Don't be so sure that what you think is going on is actually going on. Keep your secrets to yourself. A secret told is a secret no more.

2. *Dating on the job*. If you have ideas about moving up the corporate ladder, then avoid dating on the job. Very often, it is quite tempting, but it almost always leads to a dead end. Let's face it, being black makes you stand

out, so no matter what you do people will notice it. And they will talk about it. And if there is a quicker way of ending a career, it's to have "jungle fever." Since most of the people you will meet on the job will be white, consider them mine fields.

Many white men and women have heard all these wonderful and mythical things about African American sexual prowess. And there you are in an office, away from the ghetto, dressed up, looking good. That taboo and all those myths will have many of them scheming and planning to get you in bed.

The Lesson: Don't date on the job. Don't even be tempted.

3. *Drinking with the guys.* Companies always have cocktail parties, receptions, gatherings and dinners. As you've probably figured out by now, I have one philosophy about drinking: Don't do it. As long as you are in the presence of company employees, you are still at work. So it really doesn't make sense to drink on the job even if you are out of the office. It's not that you are being antisocial, it's just that as a black person, you can't afford to let your guard down. I've observed over the years at quite a few cocktail parties that someone is always taking notes. Invariably, some white person will tell you an off-color joke after their third drink. It is a lot easier to handle this behavior sober.

If you don't want to be obvious about not drinking, you can tell the bartender to bring you a water with lime or lemon in it beforehand. If a person or two teases you about not drinking, say you're allergic to alcohol and drop the subject. Large corporate meetings sometimes end with a cocktail party. While it's important to make an appearance, it's not necessary to hang out all night. So if you would like to drink a couple of beers, do it somewhere other than the cocktail party, and at some other time.

The Lesson: Party at home, with friends, not with business associates.

4. *Politics and religion.* As diverse as our society is, you can be certain that there are two subjects that people will disagree on: politics and religion. These topics carry a great deal of passion, so if you want to turn off a person for life, get on the wrong side of the discussion on either of these issues. It's a no-win situation, because there is no right. You can talk forever and never change the mind of someone who believes differently from you.

In the fifties and sixties, corporations' hiring practices started coming under fire, due in part to the preference of hiring WASPs (White Anglo-Saxon Protestants). If you think this is not true, you need only look at the presidents of America's *Fortune* 500 companies. You will see categorical exclusion based on race, religion, and sex. It was only in 1965 that Title VII became law stating that you could not discriminate.

Religion and politics go hand-in-hand in corporate America. Keep your opinions to yourself. In the work environment you are a gatherer of information, not a Democrat or Baptist trying to change the world. Corporate America's view on these two subjects clash with your being where you are anyway, so keep your nose clean by avoiding their discussion.

The Lesson: Religion and politics are not topics for conversation with colleagues.

5. *Chain of command.* As I mentioned earlier and will illustrate more fully later, corporations are modeled after the military. In the Army, you start off learning to take orders. In basic training, you are broken down both physically and mentally, and then you are built back up to be a soldier.

In military programs you do what you're told. You are

trained to react, not to think. The theory is that if you have been trained properly you will do exactly what your superior requests. Even if the person giving you that order is a jerk. Dilemma: what do you do when the orders you are given don't make sense? I can tell you for a fact that some people followed orders in Vietnam that did not make sense. In many cases, following orders meant losing their lives, and they still followed orders.

One of my close friends from college was in Khe Sahn amid some of the fiercest fighting in the war. He was with the 3rd Marine Division and had the rank of sergeant. He wrote me a letter, saying that he and his men were ordered to take a hill that meant almost sure death. The officer that gave the orders had been in the country for a very short period of time. My friend said that he protested, because he had been in Vietnam for ten months and he knew the mission to be suicide. The officer ordered him to take the hill at once. What do you think he did? What would you do?

They took the hill, and half of the platoon was wounded or killed. My friend was writing me from a hospital bed. The officer that had given the orders was one of the casualties. That's how a chain of command works: orders are passed down and followed.

Corporate America has the same rules, only you won't lose your life if you follow the orders—and you won't get any farther than you are by disobeying the rules. Being right has nothing to do with it. You simply cannot challenge, disobey, overrule, disregard, ignore, leapfrog, bypass, exclude, neglect, slight, or even badmouth your immediate supervisor and not be penalized in the corporate game. It is one of the rules in the game that remains a constant. This rule applies to everyone playing the game because without this rule there is no game.

The perception must be that you are a loyal soldier who is obedient. Webster's dictionary defines a soldier as an active, loyal, and militant follower. In corporate America, you are the soldier.

The Lesson: Rank, not the person, is the ruler.

6. *From anger to sabotage.* Once you're in the corporate world many things will happen that won't make any sense at all. Some things will have you so angry that you will want to punch somebody out. The dirty tricks, backstabbing, broken promises, and double meanings are only a few of the things you will run into if you stay around long enough. None of these things will have a damn thing to do with your being black, female, young, or old. They happen to *everyone*.

Many people try to get back at companies by sabotage. I've seen it happen so many times, and I have been around long enough to know that when you engage in sabotaging the inner workings of an organization you hurt yourself more than you really hurt the company. Even if you cost the company some money, it will keep going. Not only that, you'll make the move to another company bumpier than it need be, if you are able to move at all. Most of these companies know one another, and many of them stay in contact with one another. So if you screw up anything maliciously, other companies will know about it. This will block your path to success. Even though it's against the law to give a bad report about a former employee, it's still done, in subtle ways.

Never lose your head—in practice or in the game. As African Americans, we may find it easy to lose our heads, because we carry a lot of baggage with us into the corporate world. Emotional outbursts may cause you to be exiled from the corporate inner circle. Don't let fear drive you to hasty actions that you may regret. Remember the corporate game is a *game*, and you are a *team member*. The name of the game is to win. Think along positive lines—what you can do to better your situation, not sabotage it.

The Lesson: If the situation is impossible, just get out.

7. *Fraternizing*. In the military there is an officer's club and there is a noncommissioned officer's club. In corporate America, as in the military, officers are not supposed to fraternize with the enlisted personnel. So by design you go separate ways. Infringe on this principle even if you are invited, and you enter a political quagmire. It doesn't mix. Sometimes you develop a relationship with an officer and everything seems to be grand. Beware of the eyes that look your way while you are fraternizing.

Living on the East Coast and spending 50 percent of my time in New York, I was adopted by one of the vice presidents of the company I was working for. He brought me to New York from Chicago as his personal project, and he promoted me twice. Many times he would embarrass me by calling me into his office and asking me to close the door behind me. It was no secret that I was one of the VP's favorites. Everything was wonderful until he took another job. He left the company as part of a team to run another company.

I was open game once he left. It took me a while to figure it out, but those in ranking positions who did not share the same admiration for my work took me to task. It was a very nasty position to be in. If you have ever worked in New York as a businessperson, then you know that they invented ugly.

The Lesson: Everyone is watching with lean and hungry looks. Watch your back.

8. *Resume fever*. If you find yourself passing your resume around while still working at a company, you should

understand that there are a lot of other people doing the same thing. Passing around resumes has been going on for quite some time. One of the problems about being in an industry where there are not that many minorities is that you are easy to pick out of the crowd. And other companies will tell on you.

It is all right to have a resume on hand, but don't flaunt it. Don't pass your resume around hoping someone will fall in love with it, and you, because it won't happen. If you don't want the information getting back to your employer, then you must rely on personal contacts. Having a resume doesn't mean that you are in the direct-mail business. Never mail a resume from your office, and never have your secretary mail a resume for you. Also beware of answering blind ads—they could be from your own company!

Once you start looking for another job, your behavior changes. You're not as enthusiastic, and your head is somewhere else. Be careful in your personal contacts to let your friends know that you are open to talk, or you are always listening and approachable, but don't appear to be desperate. There is nothing that turns people off more than a desperate person. Believe me when I tell you that when someone finds out that you are desperate, you get nowhere.

Employers seldom hire from a resume alone. While I agree with the conventional wisdom that you should always have a current resume on hand, it should not be flaunted or discussed. Remember, be the best you can at what you do and people will come to you, especially headhunters (see below).

You should also join marketing clubs, speaker's bureaus, local chambers of commerce, so that you will be close to what's going on in the marketplace.

The Lesson: Be visible, not desperate. Keep your resume filed unless requested.

9. *In headhunters you trust . . . not always.* If the job is just too tough, or the promotion that was promised is not materializing, you are in the best position possible to make a move if you have been with the company for at least two years. The market loves any minority candidate who is employed with two years working experience. And a degree to boot. You're hot, and recruiters want you bad. They will offer you the moon, so be very careful in your selection, because the moon ain't theirs to give.

There will be few times in your career that you will have the luxury of being in the driver's seat. Since you are so hot, some companies will lie to you and so will some executive recruiters. In the headhunting business, the description of anyone with two to four years working experience with the same company is an MPA (Most Placeable Applicant). A recruiter will earn anywhere from $15,000 to $50,000 off your hide. Recruiters are trained to manipulate you. Most of what a recruiter says is either rehearsed or read off a piece of paper (see the script which follows). It will take a great deal of discipline on your part to be selective and not rush to the first recruiter or job that comes your way. Make sure that the company you select is a company that you want to work for, and that they have a corporate culture you can live with. Yes, it's research time again. But by now you'll have a better idea of your career path and the places where you can make that career happen.

The good headhunters know when someone has been with a company for at least two years, and they will give you a call. Be ready.

This script is used by many headhunters, and everyone who uses it on a consistent basis is in the six figures. Study the script: it is the best in the industry. It is the creation of Sandy Levy, who presently owns one of the largest employment agencies (DNA) on the West Coast. Sandy has been in the business for more than twenty years and has trained thousands of headhunters.

FADE IN: CENTURY CITY (LOS ANGELES)
EXT. SANTA MONICA BLVD. AND CENTURY PARK EAST—
MORNING

It is late summer in Los Angeles. Smoggy and hot, signaling the start of football season. The Dodgers are in last place with their worst performance ever. Emerging from the underground parking is a tall black man, walking at a fast pace toward one of the high-rise buildings. Crossing the walkway bridge to his office, he is greeted by all the familiar faces of the morning crowd. When he walks into the office, the silent whispers of "The Legend is here" travel through the office. The object of all this attention is LLOYD LINDSEY, *the twenty-six-year-old "boy wonder" graduate of UCLA, marketing manager in the executive search firm of Ferguson, Jenkins and Hazzard. He is tall, intense, and he looks fantastic in his tailored navy blue suit. He exudes confidence and charisma. Everyone in the office greets Lloyd with a smile, knowing that generates one of his patented smiles and enthusiastic "good mornings" in return.*

LINDA FERGUSON: Good morning, Lloyd.

LLOYD: Good morning, Linda. How is the firm's most valuable person?

LINDA: Wonderful, since you have been here.

Lloyd enters his office, which has a view of Beverly Hills. He hangs up his coat, puts on a headset, and pulls out a list of clients to call. He stares at the small sign just above his desk that reads: "Smile, it can be seen through the phone." He remains standing and dials a number.

LLOYD: Hi, Simret. My name is Lloyd Lindsey. How are you today?

Lloyd speaks in a conversational tone, but the words never change, especially at the beginning. This is the first checkpoint. Lloyd finds out where the person is. If he gets a negative feeling or if the person is in a meeting, he asks when he can call back.

SIMRET: Fine. What can I do for you?

LLOYD: I know you don't know me, I'm calling for an unusual reason. I'm a headhunter.

Pause . . . Another checkpoint. How do they respond? Negatively? Positively? If no response, Lloyd moves on to force a response. Otherwise, he continues in a conversational manner.

LLOYD: I take it you know what that means?

SIMRET: Yes, I do.

LLOYD: I specialize in medical sales and marketing professionals, and my client has retained me to find a particular kind of individual. Your name surfaced as a very sharp and well-informed person in our industry.

Pause . . . Another checkpoint. If no response, Lloyd forces one.

LLOYD: Is this true?

SIMRET: I've been around awhile.

LLOYD: I'd like to borrow upon your expertise for a moment and describe what I'm looking for, to see if you have any recommendations for my search. Do you have a minute now?

Another checkpoint for Lloyd. Is Simret's boss standing over her shoulder while she is talking?

SIMRET: I can't talk now.

LLOYD: Would it be better if I called you at home this

evening? What is your home number? (Pause.) Would it be better if I catch you at another time? (Pause.) When would be good? If I'm out at that time, is there a number where I can reach you this evening?

Lloyd follows his instincts. He respects her time and privacy. That's how he wins her trust and gets her home number. If she has been responding positively, Lloyd continues in his conversational manner.

SIMRET: I have just a minute, so talk to me.

LLOYD: My client is one of the top five hospital supply companies in the industry. (Sizzle) They're looking for a top-notch salesperson who is good with large hospital chains like Kaiser. A degree is required and their compensation package is second to none. Who do you know that might fit that bill?

Lloyd is now selling the job. Waiting to get a name. If he gets a name, he will ask who else she knows. Brother Lindsey is awfully shrewd, and he knows that the minute Simret inquires about the position in question, it's a buy signal. She may be asking for herself. So he answers the question and asks another question.

SIMRET: Lloyd, let's not diddle. What does the job pay?

LLOYD: Simret, it pays a base in the fifties, plus commissions of twenty to forty K. Do you think that's competitive?

SIMRET: And where might this territory be?

LLOYD: The territory is in Santa Monica. Is that the territory you cover?

SIMRET: That is my territory. OK, now give me the name of the company. I might have some interest if it's who I think it is.

LLOYD: I can't give you the name of my client because they've retained me to do the search in confidence. How do you like it at (her current company)?

SIMRET: I have no complaints.

LLOYD: You have a very good background. If I had a good position with XYZ or ABC (the best two companies), would you want to learn more about it?

This is a closing question. If Simret says yes, then Lloyd starts getting the specifics on her background, from where she went to school to her current pay. He follows up with a phone call that evening at her home. If she says no, you just know that Lloyd has some ammunition left.

SIMRET: I'm pretty happy where I am.

LLOYD: Obviously you've very happy at (her company)— it is known to be a good company. What do you like about it? (Pause.) What else? If there were one thing you could change about your current position, what would it be? Anything else?

Lloyd is finding out what Simret's hot buttons are. He listens to them instead of selling the current opening. He is winning her over. If she has loosened up, he will ask if there are any openings in her company.

SIMRET: The only thing I would change about my company is a company car. I'm tired of wearing out my own car running around.

LLOYD: If I had a position that provided a company car and was in Santa Monica, would you want me to call you about it?

Another closing question. If she says yes, Lloyd gets number.

SIMRET: Lloyd, I'm not really sure.

LLOYD: Well, I'd like to send you my card so you'll know where to reach me if you think of someone. You know how things pop up in the shower or driving the freeway! What's your address at home? And what's your number there?

Lloyd is persistent. He sends a card and says thank you

*for the help, He is legendary for flattering and pursuing
his clients. At the very least, he sends a business card. He
has fun, and the person on the other end of the line knows
that he is a real person.*

*If Lloyd gets a name from Simret, he would ask ques-
tions like these: What hospital do you call on? Who is
sharp at dealing with doctors? Who impresses you calling
on major hospitals? Who are your major competitors?
Who have you lost business to recently? Who is the salesperson you most frequently lose sales to?*

As you can see, Lloyd has Simret eating out of his hand.
If she doesn't want the position, he manages to get another name—and another possible client—from her.

Remember, a good headhunter can be your best business asset, but not until you've proven you are something
to sell. Then they will be all over you, looking to make a
commission and boost your career in the process.

10. *Mentors.* Having a mentor in corporate America is
absolutely essential for moving up the corporate ladder. A
mentor is an on-the-job teacher, guidance counselor, and
career advocate; someone who takes a liking to you, feels
you have promise, and is secure enough in their own position not to worry about you making a play for their job.
The only problem is that mentors choose you, you don't
choose them. Many brothers and sisters within the corporate structure are in positions to be mentors, but are reluctant to choose a protege—even those who want to take a
wait-and-see attitude. Part of it is protecting their own turf,
and the other part is insecurity. So even if a brother or a sister decides to give you some guidance, he or she won't do
anything until you show some promise. If you do get help,
you can believe that your mentor will be at least two steps
above you. Very few people that are only one step above

you will help you get where they are, for obvious reasons. In fact, beware of the would-be mentor just above you who promises to give you the shirt off his back. Ask yourself why he wants out of his job so badly that he's willing to teach it all to you.

There are occasions when you will have a white man or woman as a mentor, but they are few and far between. Having a mentor is obviously a big advantage, because you are not only exposed to the fine nuances of the corporate game, but you have someone behind the scenes looking out for you. Otherwise, you are like a bull in a china shop. Parts of the corporate game are so incredibly wicked there is no way that you could possibly understand them on your own (see Chapter 7). You have to have a guide. It would be like a white man walking in the 'hood during the day—it might *look* peaceful, but we know better.

So if you are lucky enough to attract a mentor, hold on for dear life. They are like gold and they choose you because they like you. And they are concerned about your growth in the company. They also see you as a good soldier. Apart from that, they get very little from it.

The Lesson: Become a good soldier and keep your eyes open for possible mentors.

11. *Burnout.* If there is anything that will bring you to your knees, it's burnout. And if you're in corporate America for too long, you will burn out and that's a fact. It is pretty frightening at first because you're not quite sure what to do. Do you seek professional help? Cash out and live in the mountains? Burnout by definition is physical or emotional exhaustion, a result of long-term stress.

When you reach that point, it is very difficult to listen to anyone because no one really knows what you are feeling at the time, and your judgment is haywire. No one understands how you can be in a funk and want relief when you seem to have it all going for you. I have talked to several businesspeople about burnout and what they have done to overcome it. The answers are as varied as world cultures. The following are some responses:

Take stock in who you are and what you want to accomplish. Ask yourself, If I could wave a magic wand, and I could do anything I wanted to, what would I be doing? What would my title be? Where would I be working? What would I do in the next year if unrestrained by money and commitment? If I only had six months to live, what would I do? What dream do I have that I pushed aside because I felt it was too unrealistic? In other words, reevaluate your goals.

The answers to these questions will give you the true power, because the fact of the matter is, you have the power to choose what you want to do with your life. Don't let life happen while you are making all kinds of other plans.

My favorite quote from the Bible is "Ask, and it shall be given you; seek, and ye shall find; knock, and it shall be opened unto you/For every one that asketh receiveth; and he that seeketh findeth; and to him that knocketh it shall be opened/Or what man is there of you, whom if his son ask bread, will he give him a stone?" (Matthew 7:7–9)

The Lesson: If a little time off doesn't heal the burnout, maybe you are doing the wrong thing. Reevaluate your goals.

12. *Racism.* There is absolutely no way to avoid racism in corporate America. It's there and it's going to stay there. The question is, what can you do to minimize its effects on you? How do you make an intolerable situation tolerable? How do you keep in check the built-in rage that

is so much a part of growing up black in America? What is the solution when statistics say that homicide is the leading cause of death for black males ages fifteen to twenty-four?

Every black person in corporate America pays some serious dues. And my hat is off to anyone presently working. You are a pioneer for black people, and you have a responsibility to leave a path for the brothers and sisters that will follow you. When I started in corporate America, there were very few black people there, and it is some twenty years later and not a whole lot has changed. There are a lot more women but there are not many more black people.

The issue is a mixed bag, and is so subtle that in some cases you are left befuddled and confused. Only through education and understanding will we remove the blatant racism that exists. I have a strange suspicion racism will swagger into the twenty-first century, rearing its ugly head at the first sign of white America's needing a scapegoat. Before Arthur Ashe died, he was asked by a reporter whether AIDS was the toughest thing he'd ever faced. Ashe replied, "No, racism is. Nothing has been more difficult than dealing with being black in America."

We have to get past going off on someone because they call us a derogatory name. It is not easy to do, but the remarks are designed to make you lose your focus. It's small-time, and there are so many other games going on you can't afford to waste your time on stupid, ignorant people. Try to keep in mind that part of the locker room mentality of corporate America makes everyone fair game when name-calling starts. If it's not race, it's religion, or politics, or body shape. And small-minded people are everywhere. You have a responsibility to rise above the little people. They are much like the basketball player that hardly plays and whose only job is to come in and use up his fouls on you. And if he can get you thrown out of the game, so much the better.

Arthur Ashe was playing in a tournament against Ilie Nastase, and Arthur was winning big, and Nastase got frustrated and blurted out, "Bloody nigger!" Arthur was near the net. He walked back to the baseline without the slightest hint of acknowledging what he had heard. Nastase roared back and ended up winning the match. When reporters asked Arthur about Nastase's abusive remark, Arthur replied, "He didn't mean anything, that's just Nastase." I remember thinking to myself at the time, Arthur, you should have verbally assaulted that no-talking Romanian. It is only in recent years that I've developed an understanding. Arthur Ashe was dealing with the bottom line. At that time it was winning, and though he lost the match he took full responsibility for losing. He had programmed himself to deal with it as an issue that would not stop him from reaching his goals.

Racism in corporate America, like society, is so pervasive that everybody in corporate America, just like everybody in society, is going to have to deal with it. That means if you are going to stay in corporate America, you are going to have to learn to deal with it. That doesn't mean that you can't fight it; you just have to fight the smart fight. Never bring racism up. When meeting it head on, don't lose your head. If you lose your head, you lose your job. If you challenge racism, you bet your job. In most cases, racism is the last card that you play. You will deal with elements of racism many times a day. It is wise to ask questions and ask questions and ask questions. But it is not wise to make accusations. Keep your head about you. Challenge everything by asking questions and demanding answers (see Sales Training, Chapter 4).

Remember that racism is so pervasive that most people are not even aware of it, even though there are two sides of it that includes people on both sides: The people who it's being perpetrated against, as well as the people who are the perpetrators. Frankly, the perpetrators usually don't view what they are doing as racism. Racism is so ingrained in us that we just assume some things about other races just as we erroneously make assumptions about men or women.

The assumption is that all blacks are in corporate America because of affirmative action, that generally blacks are not as qualified as whites. Black people as well as white people make these assumptions. We assume that Asians are smarter than other races. These are some of the stereotypes in our society, and we just deal with them on a day-to-day basis.

So what you may view as racism in certain situations may be viewed by another party as something that is just accepted. So to quickly cry "racist" is to challenge somebody who is frequently unaware of what they are doing. Corporate America is generally so competitive that people use every edge, every advantage that they might have to get ahead. And frequently we are working beside them. So many of the things that happen they do not view as being racist. That does not mean that they can go unchallenged. You can ask questions. You can ask questions as to why things were done, why decisions were made, why strategies were employed, why you may have been left out, why you may not have been included—and there is absolutely nothing unacceptable about that.

But remember, if you bring charges of racism to any situation, then you will have to prove it. If you ask questions and racism comes up as a result, then *they* have to prove it. Which is the best strategy to employ? If you want your job, you are going to have to deal with elements of racism. That doesn't mean that you have to accept it. It means that you have to work longer, harder, and smarter to disprove the ingrained stereotypes that people of other races have. When you make charges of blatant racism, you bet your career. And when you bet your career, you better be right and you better be able to prove it and you better be willing to go the distance. I believe that if you want to work in corporate America, you are going to have to know that racism is there. Just be aware and get on with your business.

Another strategy to employ in dealing with racism is to make as many friends as you can in high places or decision-making positions. That way, you will have somebody to go to to ask questions when the need arises. That's a game that you should play for many reasons. As you continue your career, the old adages "never burn bridges" and "make as many friends as you can" become important because over time your contacts are going to go places throughout the company and they may take you along. But even if they don't, you need people who can answer questions, explain situations and bring some leverage or influence to bear on certain situations that you might view as racist. The one thing you don't want to do prematurely is make that charge outright. Because once you do, you've played your trump card.

I asked several successful African-American colleagues how they dealt with racist issues on the job. Here are their responses.

TIPS FROM THE PROS

JIM CHITTY, BAXTER HEALTHCARE

How do you handle racism in the workplace?
In nineteen years working for Baxter, we have gone

through a number of cultural changes. I think the person you report to and the office that you work out of really define your experience with any company.

I formed a group in Baxter. We call ourselves the Workforce 2000 Committee. It is a minority group that includes blacks and Hispanics. The same way I deal with racism in my personal life, I deal with it in my professional life. I do something about it. You become active, you become a militant in a sense. And through our organization at Baxter we have had sensitivity training and diversity workshops. Every manager at Baxter has to go through diversity training. All the sales reps have to go through diversity training. It's a two-million-dollar program, so you work with racism constructively from an organizational sense. And also, in certain instances, you work with people who may not know any better.

I didn't have any black mentors at Baxter, but what I did was find white mentors who wanted to help me. And I grabbed on to them. There are some really good and wonderful people in all colors. And when you walk into a sales meeting or a company and you're the only black sales rep there is, someone takes an interest. There is someone who has maybe felt alone and wants to help. I personally found great role models to choose from. There were a couple of guys who believed in me and who helped me. They gave me the kind of confidence that a person needs to succeed.

Then you have certain things that happen in the work situation, like new hires who come in and are given a better territory than you. And you label it prejudice. Sometimes it is and sometimes it's not. Someone quits and the territory is divided up. You think you should have received the better accounts, but you don't. Sometimes I did and sometimes I didn't. I carried a lot of mental luggage around with me for a number of years. Not liking white people, or thinking white people were all prejudiced. Obviously, when you're in a *Fortune* 500 company, there's a glass ceiling. There's always a glass ceiling for minorities and women. But as black men, we tend to take that glass ceiling and actually *shatterproof* it. We make it worse by carrying luggage that allows us to fail. Actually, it can make us fail.

Prejudice is a hard thing to figure out, racism, overt or subtle—you're on guard. You never know if it's an act of prejudice, or if it's something that all new people go through. So sometimes your defense mechanisms get out of control. I tend now to ignore the things that I really can't pinpoint as racism. I try and think the best of people, but when I sniff it out and I find that it is racism, I'll go after it like a madman to make sure it doesn't happen again to either myself or anyone else.

So, we have to allow ourselves to break the glass ceiling. The only way you can break the glass ceiling is, number one, feel good about yourself. Number two, do the best job that you can possibly do. And number three, believe that the opportunity that you have is the best opportunity in the world.

MICHAEL THOMPSON, POLAROID CORPORATION

How do you handle racism in the workplace?
Racism is kind of a custom-made thing. Each act of racism probably requires a different response. Sometimes I ignore it, particularly when I deem that it's not something where the individual has set out to cause me harm or grievance. Let me give you an example. Years ago, I had a manufacturer's group that used to work for me, and they were located in Lubbock, Texas. I went out there to work with them after I had hired them. I was on

the elevator with this guy and he referred to me as a "good ol' boy" to some of his friends. I was offended by it, and I waited for the appropriate time to say something to him. As I was about to say something to him, a gentleman got on the elevator with us who was the president of the local bank in Lubbock, and the first guy introduced me to him. After the bank president got off the elevator, the first guy turned to me and said, "Jim is one of the good ol' boys, one of the best you ever met in your life." I understood then that this guy was not really racist: for him, it was a compliment, a term of respect. But in my culture, when you are referred to as a "boy" of any kind, it leaves a bad taste in your mouth.

We need to learn as African Americans to not respond to everything that we assume is racism. We need to examine and push back both ourselves and the individuals that may be saying this, and make sure that we understand, because everything that we hear and perceive as racist is not necessarily so.

I will give you one example that I thought was kind of comical. Years ago, an associate and I were on our way to a restaurant. There were several other Polaroid people with us in my car. The associate starting talking like Amos 'n' Andy, or like a black person using jive talk. Yessahh, boss man, yessahh—this kind of stuff. I was very angered by it. My first thought was to strike out at him, but I didn't. As we pulled up in front of this restaurant and we were about to get out of the car, I turned around to him and said, "All right, you guys, gosh my golly mannittny, let's get out of here!" He looked at me and said, "Is that the way we sound to you?" Then he added, "You made your point, man." So sometimes the best way to respond may be with a little bit of humor.

There are times when you are confronted by what I call

head-on frontal racism. Then you need to deal with it ap-
propriately and very firmly. Sometimes you may have to
reach down for some choice expletives, to let the person
know that's unacceptable behavior.

GAIL BLAKE SMITH, PACIFIC BELL

How did you handle racism in corporate America?
You have to realize especially in large corporations
that racism is inherent, it's immanent. Hopefully it
won't be so blatant that it's something that you can't
live with. My key was recognizing that it existed in the
business. Secondly, it's your *attitude.* Attitude is not a
part of the thing in life, it is the whole thing. And I was
determined not to let small-minded people be a barrier
to my success. I learned at an early age that your attitude determines your aptitude. Your attitude determines
how far you will go in the company. If I wanted to take
a militant stand and make a scene about everything that
was said and done, I clearly would not have advanced.
And I knew that. Because the people who make the decisions, as far as your success with the corporation goes,
don't want a militant.

There are certain ways that you can address things
professionally and get the attention of people without
causing conflict to the degree that it's not going to work
against you. Now, I recognize that some things I might
let go, and other things that I thought were more important, I brought to people's attention. What it would
do in the long run is get me to a position in my career
where I could really help people. And by being responsible for the hiring for Pacific Bell for Southern California, I was able to affect so much change for blacks. I
hired hundreds of black people in twelve years as the

head of human resources. Had I bit myself in the butt early on, those people probably would not be there today, and neither would I.

I can remember in 1991 one of my associates who worked in our San Francisco office, she was from Virginia. One day in front of my boss, who was Hispanic, she said, "We gotta stop hiring blacks for this work group. We need to bring in more white females." I could not believe my ears. We went on with our meeting and we finished. I went into my boss and I said, "I think my friend is clearly being racist about this hiring." I went in to talk to her about what she had said. I was pretty offended and I told her that I needed to talk to her. I explained to her that she has to be aware that I am black and I would appreciate it if she would respect me as a professional and not make certain comments. Especially in front of other people. And after she listened to me, she apologized. She said she never meant to be prejudiced or for it to come out that way. So the way I deal with it is one-on-one.

WILLIAM BURTIES, ASSISTANT VICE PRESIDENT,
UNION BANK

How do you handle racist issues on the job?
They must be handled very delicately. Earlier in my career I was working for Bank of America in Pasadena and a customer said to my face that he did not want to work with a black man. I said OK, and referred the matter to the manager of the branch. To my surprise the manager told the customer that the bank did not want his business. As far as racism on the job, I am very tactful. I always ask people to repeat themselves for clarification. And that generally is enough to disarm them. But I don't let that get in the way of my reaching my goals.

RHONDA WINDHAM, LA LAKERS

How do you handle racist issues on the job?
If someone says something I don't like, I respond. I respond in a way to educate. Ignorance is not an excuse, but it is a reason.

JOHN KELLY, PRESIDENT/CEO, ENTERPRISE
NATIONAL BANK

How do you handle racist issues on the job?
There is no good advice that I can give on how to handle racism on the job. It is certain that we live in a society where we judge a person on visual perceptions, and not on the content of one's character or ability. This is a social phenomenon that can only be fully understood when it happens to you. In retrospect, I see that I used the confrontation approach in my professional life. I found that confronting the racist with simple questions designed to play back the language used or the act perpetrated upon me was most effective. Whether they are embarrassed or angry, we certainly surprise them and therefore they can be neutralized. I believe that neutralizing racism is possible; I don't believe we can eliminate it.

PAT WATTS, SOUTHERN CALIFORNIA EDISON

How do you handle racist issues on the job?
Carefully document, document, document. Be thorough and specific with dates, times, places, and witnesses. When a pattern emerges, follow the proper procedure to elevate your concerns to your management. Careful documentation should warrant appropriate disciplinary actions against the individual. Never confront a racist, but make

sure that you give him or her notice that you expect respect in the job environment. Use kindness to combat nastiness or any other nonphysical abusive behavior.

VHONDA L. LOWRY, DIGITAL EQUIPMENT CORPORATION

How do you handle racism as a black female in corporate America?

I think you have a few options. You can either ignore it, or take it head on. I choose to confront it, deal with it, and then get beyond it. Understand that it doesn't go away—you just learn to maneuver around it.

Example: I worked in a predominately minority-run manufacturing plant. The sisters and brothers were pretty friendly and many times interacted with each other in a way that was comfortable and cultural for black folks. A white male production supervisor came to my office one day for forms. Our dialogue was friendly, with some light bantering. Then he made a comment about my backside. I told him he was out of line and he was to never speak to me in that manner again. His response was one of confusion—because he had seen the black men and women banter and exchange in a similar kind of way, he thought it was acceptable for him to do likewise, until I explained I didn't tolerate that kind of talk from anyone.

BERNARD KINSEY, CONSULTANT

How do you handle racist issues on the job?

I frankly don't deal with racism too much. In twenty-something years I really have not had a problem. I really don't deal with it. Because I know that racism is not going to keep me from where I want to go. So I don't focus on what people are trying to keep me from, I focus on what I am trying to get. And when I focus on what I'm trying to get, it's hard for somebody to spend the same amount of energy keeping me from it that I could spend in getting it. I'll give you a good example. In 1984 I awarded Jackson State University with the first million-dollar computer grant to an all-black college. I was there and the mayor of Jackson, Mississippi, came up to me and said why didn't University of Mississippi or Ole Miss receive the award. And I told him that Jackson State had a better computer science program. And then we started talking about Mississippi changing and that kind of thing. And I made the comment at the press conference that Mississippi was 48th, 49th and 50th clearly because they have spent their time keeping black folks down, and until they decide to change that, they can't get out of the ditch any quicker.

One of the things that I think summarizes what racism is: Racism is like rain; it's either gathering someplace or it's falling on you. And I just tell everybody, get your raincoat, get your umbrella, but keep getting on about your business.

The Lesson: Obstacles are the frightful things you see when you take your eyes off the goals. Keep your eye on your goal.

7

Corporate Games

*The people who get on in this world
are the people who get up and look
for the circumstances they want,
and, if they can't find them, make them.*
—GEORGE BERNARD SHAW

Corporate games are plentiful, and my purpose in writing this section is to give you a preview, uncontaminated by secondhand theory, on how black people should deal in corporate America. This section will provide you with enough information to develop your own game plan, from brothers and sisters who know firsthand what it's like to be in the trenches.

You must first understand that it is a game. A game with rules and guidelines. Be aware that you will be observed in the first year as to whether you are a team member and worthy of being on the fast track. And if you are on the fast track, management will contact you personally with probing questions: "What are your goals? What did you think of the meeting?" You will be asked to play a bigger part in meetings.

There are many ways for management to let you know that they are interested in you. If you are doing your job, the signals will be there. So keep your eyes open and your ear to the ground. On the other hand, if you are not doing the job, you will know how management feels about you. *As a rule, corporate America is about as subtle as a train wreck.*

I had a boss once who literally used to brag about not firing anyone, but instead turning the screws so tight that the person would quit on his or her own. The dangerous part about this guy was that he enjoyed seeing people sweat. He was not a people person. He was ice, as cold as they come.

When you are in the business world, you develop some close relationships. It is pretty painful when you see one of your colleagues being pushed or squeezed out of the company. The person generally tells someone so that everybody knows the details. It's the cry for help.

If you are not doing the job, you are an easy target. This particular manager was a stickler for details. So he fortified himself with the image as a hard-ass. He was a paper junkie. What I learned from him followed me throughout my career. He was the toughest manager I have ever been associated with. To top the whole thing off, as if being six-two and weighing two-hundred pounds were not enough, this white dude was a black belt in karate. So he kept your anger at arm's length.

You may not meet anyone as ruthless, but you will meet someone who will come after you at some time or another. What you do will shape your career, and decide its length in the business world. Listed below are some of the games businesspeople play.

THE EARLY MORNING BREAKFAST

The early morning breakfast is one of the oldest games in the book. It serves to aggravate you, but it is really designed to take you out of your comfort zone. If a manager decides that he or she wants to see you for a meeting at 7 A.M. instead of the usual 8 A.M., you know something's up. If you go to the meeting with a long face, not only will you make the manager's day, you will probably make their week. Which means that you can expect more early morning meetings.

You should own that game anytime it's played on you. My philosophy was to beat my boss to the spot and have already had a cup of coffee. And I would greet him with enthusiasm, and delight in the meeting, because the general premise is to go over some figures, or to discuss some new strategy. So accept it as help and be grateful. Have plenty of questions to ask so that when you leave the meeting, you have planted the seed that this was fun. Free breakfast and free advice. What have I done to receive such wonderful attention?

Write a follow-up note to your boss thanking him or her for the help. Let your boss know that you really appreciate their giving you direction. Let your boss know that you look forward to meeting again for an early morning breakfast. After all, you got a great start that morning. You might have a tough time the first time you do this, but arrange your day accordingly.

Put on a happy face, because this is the easiest of the games. And everyone plays it, so prepare yourself for it. Once your boss backs off, be mindful not to throw your victory in his or her face. It is a victory only you can savor, because should your boss get wind of your telling someone, your meetings might end up resembling Army boot camp.

This is one of the games that requires *going to the mat*. It is one of the many war games that requires special mental preparation.

INTIMIDATION

One of the biggest games is intimidation. People in corporate America will try and intimidate you to gain an edge in dealing with you. The intimidation could be to get you to do more work. In many cases, it is to get you to side with whoever is doing the intimidating. Basically the game is designed to control you.

Many of the tricks that intimidators use in asserting themselves involve access to information. Information that these people may or may not have. As an example, they will say something like "I was talking to someone in the organization and they said that they didn't think that you were a real team player or they no longer view you very positively." These people attempt to intimidate you with their supposed access to information that you don't have. They want you to assume that they are closer to someone in the company that has decision-making power. If you believe that and you are willing to listen to them, they can control you.

PIGGYBACK

The piggyback game is one where your work has someone else's name attached to it: taking credit for the work but not taking responsibility for it. When a project comes from your department, a piggybacker wants his or her name attached to it but doesn't want to take responsibility for it. If it's a success, these people want credit. If it fails, they don't want the acknowledgment or association. They ride on your back so that you carry the load. They position themselves to jump off only when convenient.

I was involved in a major project that was somewhat

of a long shot to pull off. There were several people involved, and if one person dropped the ball, we would not be able to pull the project off. Since I had a connection with the key person, I just assumed that I would enjoy the success if we pulled it off. Not only was I excluded, but I was told to my face by the person taking credit that he did it all by himself. But the most frustrating part about this particular project was that I had been told by colleagues not associated with it to watch out for the very thing that happened.

There will be many people wanting to take credit but not responsibility.

THE SLOWDOWN

The mental games are not restricted to those who are not doing the job. In many cases the games are designed to see if you are a soldier. You could be doing a bang-up job, but the overriding question will still be one of the following: Can he or she be one of the guys or gals? Is he or she someone that we will enjoy hanging out with? Will he or she be *our* soldier?

You can expect that sometime within a two-year period, someone will test you. If a manager has promised you something, and his or her manager doesn't like you, you don't get promoted. Some organizations have what they call an "open door policy." If you complain, even though you have a legitimate gripe, the slowdown can be employed. Your manager will know where the chink is in your armor, because that's his job. If you are habitually late with your paperwork, even though you have great numbers, that is the first flank that they will attack.

Your first sign will be a memo to you about the importance of having your paperwork in on time. The memo is written not so much to let you know that your paperwork is late, as it is to start a file on you. A copy of the letter will go to another manager as a cc (copy sent to) or bc (blind copy). The way you answer is crucial. Because if you are bitter, they have won, and they direct from then on.

Corporations are paperwork factories: one half is covering their ass, and the other half is kicking ass. All with paper. If you exaggerate on your expense account, are late on paperwork, or have a problem with someone else, it will be a flank open to attack. You can fight, ride it out, or look for another job. Just don't ask for a promotion. Paper is a sure way to slow you down.

HOME GAMES

Work does not end at the job, or job site. If you become a target—for whatever reason—you can expect phone calls at home. A mistake made by many is considering home as a sanctuary to retreat to. Home as seen by corporate America is just another branch office. It's where you have your files, PC, and other office equipment. And it is the one place where most people have their guard down.

There has to be a time when you sit down and relax with your family. If you have made all your calls, and have the following day planned out, then put the answering machine on. In other words, screen your calls. Nothing is worse than being blindsided by a call the purpose of which is to disrupt you with a different plan for the next day.

*Genius is one percent inspiration
and ninety-nine percent
perspiration.*
—THOMAS EDISON

FIVE ON ONE

A friend who has worked in the upper echelons of corporate America was talking to me about some dirty tricks. We were talking about basketball, and he just burst out laughing. He said, "You know the corporate game has a play called five on one?" With a puzzled look, I asked what he was talking about. He said that some executives will write a series of memos; five of them will get to their intended target and one will not. The sixth memo is never intended to arrive. The executive keeps copies, and it is the victim (the person to whom the memos are directed) who determines whether the fake memo will be used. If the receiving party is not conscientious, then he or she will eventually get hammered by failure to respond to a memo that was never received.

Example: If something has gone wrong in the business arena and someone has to cover his or her ass, the memo writer holds the nonexistent memo as a trump card to be played at the precise moment. When there is a meeting with a mediator to straighten things out so to speak, the question invariably asked by the mediator is "Well, why didn't you address this problem earlier, Jerry?" To which the memo writer responds, "I did." The setup, of course, is that the unsuspecting memo recipient has not the slightest clue that he is a part of the five on one and rightfully disagrees. At which time the memo writer plays the trump card, the memo that was never sent. If you are the least bit unorganized, you are zapped!

RELOCATION

I have yet to discern the logic of a man or woman living in Los Angeles, unemployed with a family, and not taking a job in another state. It's absolutely ludicrous, because at some time or another you are going to be asked to move. That is, if you are working for corporate America. Businesspeople are falling all over themselves to make a living in Los Angeles, when many of them can take their talent to another state and live like kings and queens. Moving is an intricate part of the game in corporate America. It's the rule across the board, unwritten but very important to survival in the corporate game. Relocating shows a willingness to play the game, and in this game one of the cardinal rules is this: Put the Corporation First. Failure to do this it is the easiest way to be got rid of, or prevented from moving up.

Managers find out beforehand what your feelings are about moving. When you express an unwillingness to move, you can bet at some time a promotion will come *requiring* you to move. Once you refuse, you are disqualified.

One of my friends works for a high-profile blue-chip company, and he was one of the top marketing managers in the country for nine out of ten years, exceeding all objectives, literally adding millions to the bottom line. He refused a promotion at the five-year mark, and he was put on the shelf. He finally became frustrated seeing his white counterparts leapfrog him with less experience and inferior numbers. He inquired about the obvious exclusion, and the response was, "We didn't know you were interested in upper management." After much ado, he was promoted.

GOING TO THE MAT

If you receive an evaluation performance review, or MBO (management by objective) that is not favorable, it is a clear sign your job with the company is on the line. Evaluations are designed to build a case in writing either good or bad. Anything less than above average puts you on the bubble. Meaning that you will have to fight like crazy just to keep your head above water.

Your immediate boss is either for you or against you. I have yet to see one in between. If your manager wants you to improve, he or she will provide you with the strategy for getting ahead. The review will be above average as long as your boss is in your corner. Average means that the reviewer is indifferent, which does very little for your career.

Going to the mat means protecting your career, taking a negative and turning it into a positive. Initiate a meeting with your boss on how you can improve your situation. Whatever you do, don't start moping.

Since you are developing a strategy to get back on track, you can start by sending memos to your boss asking for help. Each memo is designed for a response, a cry for help if you will. You have to be asking for something that you need. If you don't have a well-designed plan for your own success, this scenario will blow up in your face. If you are certain that you are going to leave the company, going to the mat buys you time.

Once you decide to make a move, you will need help. I suggest you hire a part-time secretary, if possible. If you try and make a move to another company without help, you will become so frustrated you will end up quitting before you find another job. Otherwise you end up with the leper quality: you must have a job when looking; otherwise no one will want to come near you.

Don't get frustrated. Set up a three-month plan and a six-month plan for getting a job. Success lies in keeping your head.

> *Feeling sorry for yourself and your present*
> *condition is not only a waste of*
> *energy, but the worst habit*
> *you could possibly have.*
> —DALE CARNEGIE

LETTER OF RESIGNATION

Always give your employer two weeks' notice. In order to document this, always date your letter in the upper right-hand corner in such a way as to reflect a two-week gap between the date the letter is submitted and the date of resignation. The following is a sample letter of resignation. Always resign on a Friday.

Garrett Morgan   Friday, July 16, 1993
Gas Mask Lights Company
Washington, D.C.

Dear Mr. Morgan,

After very careful consideration, I have decided to accept another opportunity. This difficult decision was based upon both personal and career needs, and should not be interpreted in a negative manner.

On the contrary, I have the highest regard for Gas Mask Lights and my associates here. I have thoroughly enjoyed my term of employment with the firm and will remember my association with GML fondly.

It is therefore with some regret but firm resolve that I hereby inform you that, effective as of today, I am giving two weeks' notice, and that Friday, July 30, 1993, will be my last day of employment.

This decision is final and irrevocable, and once again is based solely and exclusively upon personal and career considerations.

Sincerely,
Donna King

cc: (supervisor's boss)

AGE

If you are not locked into a company by the age of thirty-six, you had better be carrying some mean credentials. Corporate America is just not interested in employees over thirty-six—not just blacks but people in general. Unless you are specialized in something, the feeling is that it's a waste of time to try and change you. It's a real tricky area, so you must be really careful if you decide to make the move from one company to another. If you do make the move, make sure that you research the company, and know something about the company's direction. If you look closely enough, you will get a feeling as to what the company is up to. Don't be afraid to ask for a two-year contract in writing.

One of the toughest jobs in the recruiting business is telling a friend that you can't do anything for him or her when he or she has a lot of good experience. But corporations discriminate not only by color, but by age as well. The feeling is that you should be in upper management when you are in your thirties, but the catch is that if you're black that is both more difficult and more stringently applied.

A brother who is an acquaintance of mine spent several years in corporate America as a regional vice president, then took a job as vice president of a major toy company. The difference was that in the first company he had regional responsibility, and in the company he went to he was VP of the company. It was a grand move for a brother in this day and age, but he wasn't there for a year before the company folded. This was a well-known toy company, and yet as astute as my acquaintance was as a businessman, he was burned. As happy as we were when he got the gig, our mouths were agape when the bad news came. (It was like, shouldn't he have known?) It worked out well for him in the end, because since no one (well, almost no one) hires a black ex-VP at the advanced age of thirty-eight, he went into business for himself and is doing much better financially than he would have even if the toy company had stayed in business.

It is sort of a joke in the industry the number of resumes in recruiting offices of people over thirty-six who are unemployed. When a candidate is hot, a company will pay in the neighborhood of $45,000 for him or her. They won't give you a nickel for someone over the mark. Don't get me wrong—you can get a job, just not in the *Fortune* 500 companies. Unless, of course, you know someone, but that scenario generally eludes brothers and sisters.

THE DOWNSIZING GAME

The downsizing game is to get people to quit or leave the company without going through all the formal terms and conditions of the downsizing project. If they can get you to quit voluntarily, then it makes their job a lot easier. It could be that there is somebody else that they would prefer to keep.

Without having to provide you with an explanation that would be difficult to digest, someone will give you all the reasons that you should leave. And the conversation will sound like this person is doing you this big favor. Example: "You know, Elbert, it's going to happen anyway; it's coming and it would probably make more sense for you if you left under your own terms. The truth of the matter is that those who are left are going to be subject to three and in some cases five times the work that was expected before. Therefore, it makes sense to just resign. You will be a lot better off than those of us who stay."

If you buy that, then they don't have to explain to you all the formal conditions of the contract. Only because you left voluntarily. Be aware of that, because you also leave money on the table.

THINKING IN MILITARY TERMS

"Greetings from the President of the United States" is how the letter read when I was drafted into the U.S. Army in 1967. At that time, being drafted meant that you were almost certain to be going to Vietnam. From being one happy camper in my senior year of college, I became a very frightened person just by opening the letter. By October 1968, I found myself in Long Binh, Vietnam.

Long Binh was very popular among soldiers, and was known as LBJ (Long Binh Jail). It was a military fortress. When Bob Hope arrived for the Christmas holidays with Ann-Margret and other guests, he called Long Binh "Vietnam's answer to Hollywood." Once settled in, you adapted as best you could, but you adapted nonetheless. The 60's being what they were, you became observant of your surroundings. War forces you to become an active participant in your own survival.

The Army first sent me to Fort Ord, California, which is located in the northern part of the state near Monterey, on the beach. At the center for new draftees, there's a waiting center where you do all your testing and get your shots, haircut, physical, and Army gear. It is also the place that the cliques are formed. I found myself hooked up with two brothers from Watts and this white hippie dude name Dailey, who was from Long Beach, California. The four of us stood in a corner and stared at the rest of the group, carrying around the frown that left only when you put food in it. It was absolute craziness watching some one hundred recruits in a two-story building with space so cramped you could hear conversations on the other side of the room. The four of us made a pact that we would talk among ourselves, volunteer nothing, and watch one another's backs.

In the meantime, the military started doing what they have obviously been doing for hundreds of years: breaking the raw recruits down to be soldiers. But a strange thing happened. Out of the blue another recruit came running upstairs asking for me, hollering as if he were a high school cheerleader. "Wilson, the sergeant wants to see you, the sergeant wants to see you!" I followed him down the steep, narrow staircase, and he was saying, "You're going to be the acting sergeant on the hill!" Once in the drill sergeant's cubbyhole, he blurted out, "You're going to be the trainee leader on the hill!" The drill sergeant said that I would have the power of a real sergeant. My responsibilities would include making out a duty roster for everything having to do with my barracks, from the cleaning of the barracks to assigning KP (kitchen patrol). I would be the only one with my own room and no physical duties. My job would be to see that assignments were carried out. After the sergeant gave me the rundown on what my responsibilities were, he said that he wanted to know one thing: "I want to know if you can jump on a black guy as fast as you can jump on a white guy." Without hesitating I said, "Yes." The sergeant grabbed my hand and said, "Then the job is yours."

I felt pretty weird about how easily I was seduced, but took my news to the fellas right away. My new position was given a great deal of resistance, even though we had spent the previous ten days doing some serious bonding. Without my saying a word, they told me that I had sold out, and that I had become a part of the system that we were so opposed to. In unison, the three of them turned their backs on me. When an opportunity for reasoning was granted, I asked one question: "What would you rather have, one of the many jerks whose faces we've been in give you orders, or would you rather have me making the assignments as to who has KP on the weekends, or who cleans up the latrine and waxes the floor?" In short, I made them an offer they couldn't refuse.

I thought the four of us were out of the loop completely, but this was war, and the Army knew all along what they were doing. On the hill, there were exactly thirty-two of us in my platoon, three brothers including myself, and the rest white. Of those, seventeen of them were from Tennessee and they were all in the National Guard. This meant that after basic training they went home, while the rest of us had an 80 percent chance of going to Vietnam. My point is that there were a few men in the group who were bigger than I was, and there were several who knew a hell of a lot more about the military and its protocol, but they picked the bandit to run the show.

The personalities in this situation were varied, as you would imagine, from one guy in my platoon who was six-foot-two, weighing 240 pounds, with the facade of a leader of the Hell's Angels, to a very skinny young guy who in his early days pissed on himself because he was afraid to ask for permission to go to the latrine on the shooting range. What impressed me about this whole scenario was that the first week on the hill, we looked like the worst bunch of misfits that you can imagine. In one way it was funny, and in another we all knew that we were getting primed for the war.

Out of all of this, the one person who I was most impressed with was the young man named Dennis that wet on himself. At the end of the eight weeks, he had added about fifteen pounds and he stood taller. At our graduation from basic, his mother came up to him and said, "My little baby!" and he instinctively retorted, "Mother, don't call me a baby, because I'm a man!" So dramatic was the turnaround of Dennis, it was hard not to realize that there is a method to the Army madness. It is the cleverest form of brainwashing that you can imagine.

Corporate America is so much like it, I found it necessary to write this section to try and give you a better understanding of what you are coming up against. If you don't understand these dynamics, you will be so completely lost that you might as well go and pick up your grocery basket and start collecting bottles and cans to get a head start on being homeless.

In one of my conversations with Ed Barker, the vice

president of Sony, I asked what he had to do to get the
job and what was required. One of the requirements
was to read *A Book of Five Rings* by Miyamoto Musashi. The book is about a Samurai warrior in the six-
teenth century who fought and killed more than sixty
men before he was thirty years old. In one of his earliest
fights as a teenager, he beat an experienced warrior to
death with a stick. The warrior had a sword and was
still beaten to death. Musashi goes on kicking everybody's ass until he is satisfied that he is invincible. Musashi was single-minded in perfecting his skill, to the
point of not bathing so that at no time would he be
without his weapon. Single-mindedness, being focused,
surviving: this book is one of the more popular books
among businessmen. Every time I see a Japanese businessman bowing, I can only think of Musashi, Western
ways of thinking, and strategy.

Reading *A Book of Five Rings* led me to read *The Art
of War for Executives* by Donald Krause. Krause has
done an excellent job of breaking down the original
work *The Art of War* by Sun Tzu. Understand that we
are talking about a piece of work on war that was gen-
erated some twenty-five hundred years ago. It is a lot
easier to digest Krause, so I would start with that version first. I suggest that you buy and read all three
books. Most business students read them as a require-
ment for graduation.

Once you understand that the structures of corporate
America and the military are pretty much the same, you
are less likely to build your corporate career on sandcas-
tles. It is not unusual for the heads of countries, presidents of corporations, and head coaches to read and use
information and advice from military leaders. One of the
most famous of these leaders was Napoleon Bonaparte

of France, and one of his chief rivals was the German philosopher and war strategist General Karl von Clausewitz. When Clausewitz asked Bonaparte why men go to war, Bonaparte replied, "Men go to war because the women are watching."

If you find a quote, a note, a nugget, an idea or a scenario that you can relate to, pass it on to another brother or sister. Our struggle is to share information.

8

Reaching for
the Corner Office

A new generation of African Americans is moving into the work force. There are more men and women of color in decision-making positions than at any other time in corporate America's history. Yet the "glass ceiling" remains as the invisible shield that turns back the larger force seeking to obtain a spot in the corner office. It is so pervasive that in 1990 the government created the federal Glass Ceiling Commission. After four years of study, the Glass Ceiling Commission said that blacks face the most barriers of anyone to promotion up the corporate ladder. As if that was not enough, Robert Reich, labor secretary and commission chairman, after going over the figures of fifteen hundred of the country's biggest companies, determined that 97 percent of senior managers were white males. Mr. Reich's response was that "serious barriers" existed in corporate America. Mmmmm. I could have told Mr. Reich that. The report also said that white men received mentoring and other support automatically from other white men.

The time is now for brothers and sisters to make the move to that corner office. If we leave it up to some commission, we will hear more about the problems, but no one comes up with a solution. We are just learning to play the game. We are closing in on the twenty-first century and only now people are telling us that there are rules. From the many conversations that I have had with our brothers and sisters who have shattered the glass ceiling, I have distilled what should be your road map to the corner office.

MENTORING

Connecting with a mentor is obviously very important. But the question still remains: how do you get one? If you are not chosen, does that mean that you are left to fend for yourself? Not everyone is interested in the corner office—with the corner office comes a great deal of responsibility, accountability, and obligation.

When I first arrived in Chicago with Levi Strauss & Co., I made a point of observing the best marketing representative in the office. There were two men who were making more than $100,000 a year, and I observed both making presentations. I picked the one that I felt most comfortable with. I let him know that I valued his advice, and expressed my willingness to assist him in any way that I could. He in turn became my teacher, counselor, and friend. With his help, in less than a year I was promoted twice and ended up having the responsibility in Philadelphia that my mentor had in Chicago.

The situations will be different no matter where you go

or who you work for. We can have mentors younger than we are, from whom we can learn a great deal. We can also have peers as mentors. The purpose of mentors is to learn; race or gender should not be a factor. Ideally what you want from a mentor is good advice on career goals, increased visibility, encouragement, and enhanced growth opportunities. When you select a mentor, or if you are selected, ask yourself if this is the kind of help you need.

GOAL SETTING

I can't say enough about goal setting because it is the one area most neglected. Commit your goals to writing. This makes them more believable and attainable. If it's your goal to be vice president of marketing or president of the company, write it down. It's then easier to track your progress and harder to deny the existence of your goals. You will probably want to have a two-year plan, a five-year plan, and a ten-year plan. Once you commit to achieving your goals, you are well on your way. It may be that as you start moving toward a goal, you decide it's not really what you want. That's no problem, because you can change. The important thing is to have some direction.

How do you see your lifestyle? Do you want to live in a large house overlooking the city or ocean? What about vacation? Where would your ideal vacation be? What are five things that motivate you? What are the five areas of business that motivate you? If you could wave a magic wand, what would your job title be? Where would you be working? What are your job fantasies? To have some purpose and create excitement, you need to answer these questions truthfully. Your personal goals will make the job goals easier to achieve. Goal setting is simple, but it is not easy.

PROMOTIONS

I interviewed and talked to a number of brothers and sisters about being promoted, and how to negotiate the best deal. How do you know when a promotion is due you? And what do you do if you think you're being overlooked for a promotion? Surprisingly, some of those I interviewed wanted to be off the record, because of what's going on in corporate America today. But the consensus seems to be that if you feel that you are being overlooked for a promotion, you must take the most direct route, which is generally your immediate supervisor, and ask why you were overlooked.

One of the brothers who I interviewed worked for a company that has an open door policy, meaning that you can make your grievance known, as long as you let your supervisor know that's what you plan to do. He went to the executive with all of his documented achievements and made his case. His problem was that his immediate supervisors were being promoted at such a rapid pace that he could not develop any rapport for his own agenda. The executive listened, and in less than six months the brother was promoted to the marketing manager's position that he had been seeking. He proved himself to be a very valuable player in the corporate game. His advice is to meet the problem head on. Ask questions. He asked questions, and negotiated a better deal.

If you have set goals for yourself, the rule is to discuss them with your boss. What should I be doing to reach the position of product manager or director of marketing? Between your boss and your mentor, you will develop your own road map to your desired position. You have your time lines and corporate America has theirs. In a great many cases, your desired goals will be achieved at another company. But only you can find that out.

THE TEN COMMANDMENTS OF BUSINESS SURVIVAL

To borrow from the great poet Rudyard Kipling, if you can keep your head when all about you are losing theirs, you're ahead of the game. If you follow these steps, you will have all you will ever need to succeed in corporate America.

1. IF YOU OFFER ANYONE A GUARANTEE, MAKE SURE IT'S ON AN ASPECT OF THE BUSINESS THAT IS ROUTINELY PERFORMED.
2. IF YOU LEARN TO HANDLE REJECTION, HANDLING SUCCESS WILL BE A SNAP.
3. IF YOU'RE INTERESTED IN OBTAINING SOMETHING FROM SOMEONE ELSE, ALWAYS PREFACE YOUR REQUEST WITH "I HAVE A FAVOR TO ASK OF YOU." PEOPLE HATE TURNING DOWN FAVORS.
4. IF YOU HAVE TO TELL YOUR BOSSES BAD NEWS, MAKE SURE YOU CALL THEM BEFORE THEY CALL YOU.
5. IF YOU'VE MADE A MISTAKE WITH AN ORDER OR CORRESPONDENCE, ADMIT IT QUICKLY AND BE DONE WITH IT,
6. IF YOU EXERCISE DURING YOUR LUNCH HOUR, IT MAKES YOUR AFTERNOON TWICE AS PRODUCTIVE.
7. IF YOU MAKE YOUR IMPORTANT CALLS

IN THE MORNING AND YOU RETURN PHONE CALLS BETWEEN 4:30 P.M. AND 5:30 P.M., YOU WILL BE MAKING THE MOST EFFECTIVE USE OF THE TELEPHONE.

8. IF YOU ASSOCIATE WITH THE TOP PERFORMERS IN YOUR GROUP, YOU NEED ONLY MODEL THEIR SUCCESS TO BE SUCCESSFUL.

9. IF YOU REHEARSE WHAT YOU ARE GOING TO SAY DURING A PRESENTATION AND YOU KNOW WHAT YOU WANT TO ACCOMPLISH, YOU HAVE PREPARED TO MAKE AN EFFECTIVE PITCH!

10. IF AN ASSOCIATE IS ANGRY, LET THAT ASSOCIATE HAVE HIS OR HER SAY WITHOUT INTERRUPTION. THEN WRITE THE COMPLAINTS AND NUMBER THEM ON A SHEET OF PAPER. PROBLEMS ON PAPER ARE NEVER AS LARGE AS THEY ARE IN YOUR HEAD.

TIPS FROM THE PROS

VHONDA L. LOWRY, DIGITAL EQUIPMENT CORPORATION

What advice would you give young men and women today regarding getting promoted and breaking the glass ceiling?

- Determine what game is being played and whose agenda is being worked.
- Find out who is in the position of power, that is, "political" and "organizational" power (they're the ones that you influence or who are influential).

- Go where they go, do what they do (golf), be positioned so that you can have a dialogue with them on the things that they like to do and they like to discuss, etc.
- Have your support network of both minority and non-minority. People should be saying good things about you when your name comes up. Learn from them.

Having visibility with people who are in decision-making positions is important. It certainly was for me. I worked for a lot of bosses, but I tried to work for bosses that were respected and whose senior management would listen. Because these are the people that will be your mentors and will help support you. Mentors are a must today.

BERNARD KINSEY, CONSULTANT

What advice would you give young men and women today regarding getting promoted and breaking the glass ceiling?

One of the first things to do is network. At Xerox we had one of the most powerful employee networks in the country. The reason that we were successful is that back twenty years ago we decided we were going to change the face of Xerox, and we worked extremely well. Seventy men and women took that approach and it really worked. And what you have to do is ask yourself, What skills do I bring to this, and which ones do others bring that are even better? And begin to help each other develop those complimentary and associated skills so that you can push and pull each other up.

PAT WATTS, SOUTHERN CALIFORNIA EDISON

What advice would you give young men and women today regarding getting promoted and breaking the glass ceiling?

Today, problems in the workplace are not much different than they were thirty years ago. African Americans are still being denied the right to compete. I suggest perseverance and determination. If you continue to show that you are determined to meet your goals, that you have performed as well as anybody and you will not be defeated, eventually they will give you a chance. Learn the politics of the organization. Understand the corporate strategic direction and be able to articulate and discuss it knowledgeably at any time.

WILLIAM BURTIES, ASSISTANT VICE PRESIDENT, UNION BANK

What advice would you give young men and women today regarding getting promoted and breaking the glass ceiling?

Breaking the glass ceiling is still one of the toughest barriers. My advice is to identify your weakness and work on it. And make sure that the path that you are taking leads you to the corner office.

RHONDA WINDHAM, LA LAKERS

What advice would you give young men and women today regarding getting promoted and breaking the glass ceiling?

You must work twice as hard. Find a mentor within the organization. Keep your personal life separate. Don't screw where you work. For the ladies, better to be one of the guys than anything else. I think too much emphasis is on promotion within a company. We should strive to start our own companies. *Network!!! Network!!! Network!!!*

JOHN KELLY, PRESIDENT/CEO, ENTERPRISE NATIONAL BANK

What advice would you give young men and women today regarding getting promoted and breaking the glass ceiling?

Start your own business. I believe that young African Americans need to wake up and smell the coffee. White America is not going to help you take over their position of power in our society. You must do that for yourself. By sheer numbers, people of color will comprise the majority in the world by the year 2000. Yet about economic and social empowerment, the races are not prepared to do anything with the power they have in their numbers. Understanding and working within the free enterprise system is key to economic empowerment.

When African Americans begin to dream dreams and see visions of ownership rather than employment opportunities, then they can look up and there will be no glass ceiling.

> *When you cannot make up your mind which of two evenly balanced courses of action you should take, choose the bolder.*
> —GENERAL W. J. SLIM

SPORTS FRANCHISE DIRECTORY

Pro Basketball

Atlanta Hawks
One CNN Center, South Tower, Suite #405
Atlanta, GA 30303
(404) 827-3800

Boston Celtics
161 Merrimac Street
Boston, MA 02114
(617) 523-6050

Charlotte Hornets
One Hive Drive
Charlotte, NC 28217
(704) 357-0252

Chicago Bulls
980 N. Michigan Avenue, Suite #1600
Chicago, IL 60611
(312) 943-5800

Cleveland Cavaliers
The Coliseum
2933 Streetsboro Road
Richfield, OH 44286
(216) 659-9100

Dallas Mavericks
Reunion Arena
777 Sports Street
Dallas, TX 75207
(214) 748-1808

Denver Nuggets
McNichols Sports Arena
1635 Clay Street
Denver, CO 80204
(303) 893-6700

Detroit Pistons
The Palace of Auburn Hills
Two Championship Drive
Auburn Hills, MI 48326
(313) 377-0100

Golden State Warriors
Oakland Coliseum Arena
Oakland, CA 94621
(510) 638-6300

Houston Rockets
The Summit
Ten Greenway Plaza
Houston, TX 77046
(713) 627-0600

Indiana Pacers
300 E. Market Street
Indianapolis, IN 46204
(317) 263-2100

Los Angeles Clippers
L.A. Memorial Sports Arena
3939 S. Figueroa Street
Los Angeles, CA 90037
(213) 748-8000

Los Angeles Lakers
Great Western Forum
3900 West Manchester Blvd.
Inglewood, CA 90306
(310) 419-3100

Miami Heat
The Miami Arena
Miami, FL 33136-4102
(305) 577-4328

Milwaukee Bucks
The Bradley Center
1001 N. Fourth Street
Milwaukee, WI 53203-1312
(414) 227-0500

Minnesota Timberwolves
600 First Avenue North
Minneapolis, MN 55403
(612) 673-1600

National Basketball Association
645 Fifth Avenue
New York, NY 10022
(212) 826-7000

National Basketball Association Players Association
1775 Broadway, Suite #2401
New York, NY 10019
(212) 333-7510

New Jersey Nets
Meadowlands Arena
East Rutherford, NJ 07073
(201) 935-8888

New York Knickerbockers
Madison Square Garden
Two Pennsylvania Plaza
New York, NY 10121-0091
(212) 465-6499

Orlando Magic
One Magic Place
Orlando Arena
Orlando, FL 32801-1114
(407) 649-3200

Philadelphia 76ers
Veterans Stadium
Box 25040
Philadelphia, PA 19147-0240
(215) 339-7600

Phoenix Suns
America West Arena
Box 1369
Phoenix, AZ 85001
(602) 266-5753

Portland Trail Blazers
Memorial Coliseum
700 N.E. Multnomah Street, Suite 600
Portland, OR 97232
(503) 234-9291

Sacramento Kings
Arco Arena
One Sports Parkway
Sacramento, CA 95834
(916) 928-0000

San Antonio Spurs
HemisFair Arena
600 E. Market Street, Suite 102
San Antonio, TX 78205
(512) 554-7787

Seattle Supersonics
The Coliseum
190 Queen Anne Avenue North, Suite 200
Seattle, WA 98109
(206) 281-5800

Utah Jazz
Delta Center
301 West So. Temple
Salt Lake City, UT 84180
(206) 575-7800

Washington Bullets
Capital Centre
One Harry S. Truman Drive
Landover, MD 20785
(301) 773-2255

Pro Football

National Football League Players Association
202 L Street N.W.
Washington, D.C. 20036
(202) 463-2200

Canadian Football League
110 Eglinton Avenue West, 5th Floor
Toronto, Ontario M4R 1A3, CAN
(416) 322-9650

World League of American Football
540 Madison Avenue
New York, NY 10022
(212) 838-9400

NATIONAL CONFERENCE

Atlanta Falcons
Georgia Dome
I-85 and Suwanee Road
Suwanee, GA 30174
(404) 945-1111

Chicago Bears
250 N. Washington Road
Lake Forest, IL 60045
(708) 295-6600

Dallas Cowboys
One Cowboy Parkway
Irving, TX 75063
(214) 556-9900

Detroit Lions
1200 Featherstone Road
Pontiac, MI 48342
(313) 335-4131

Green Bay Packers
1265 Lombardi Avenue
Green Bay, WI 54307-0628
(414) 496-5700

Los Angeles Rams
2327 W. Lincoln Avenue
Anaheim, CA 92801
(714) 535-7267

Minnesota Vikings
9520 Viking Drive
Eden Prairie, MN 55344
(612) 828-6500

National Football League
410 Park Avenue
New York, NY 10022
(212) 758-1500

New Orleans Saints
1500 Poydras Street
New Orleans, LA 70112
(504) 733-0255

Philadelphia Eagles
Veterans Stadium
Box 25050
Philadelphia, PA 19148
(214) 463-2500

Phoenix Cardinals
Box 888
Phoenix, AZ 85001-0888
(602) 379-0101

San Francisco 49ers
4949 Centennial Boulevard
Santa Clara, CA 95054
(408) 562-4949

Tampa Bay Buccaneers
One Buccaneer Place
Tampa, FL 33607
(813) 870-2700

Washington Redskins
Redskins Park
Box 17247/Dulles International Airport
Washington, D.C. 20041

AMERICAN CONFERENCE

Buffalo Bills
One Bills Drive
Orchard Park, NY 14127
(716) 648-1800

Cincinnati Bengals
200 Riverfront Stadium
Cincinnati, OH 45202
(513) 621-3550

Cleveland Browns
80 First Street
Berea, OH 44017
(216) 891-5000

Denver Broncos
13655 Broncos Parkway
Englewood, CO 80112
(303) 649-9000

Houston Oilers
6910 Fannin Street
Houston, TX 77030
(713) 797-9111

Indianapolis Colts
Box 535000
Indianapolis, IN 46253
(317) 297-2658

Kansas City Chiefs
One Arrowhead Drive
Kansas City, MO 64129
(816) 924-9300

Los Angeles Raiders
332 Center Street
El Segundo, CA 90245
(310) 322-3451

Miami Dolphins
Joe Robbie Stadium
2269 N.W. 199th Street
Miami, FL 33056
(305) 620-5000

New England Patriots
Foxboro Stadium
Route 1
Foxboro, MA 02035
(508) 543-8200

New York Jets
1000 Fulton Avenue
Hempstead, NY 11550
(516) 538-6600

Pittsburgh Steelers
Three Rivers Stadium
300 Stadium Circle
Pittsburgh, PA 15212
(412) 323-1200

San Diego Chargers
Jack Murphy Stadium
Box 609609
San Diego, CA 92160-9609
(619) 280-2111

Seattle Seahawks
11220 N.E. 53rd Street
Kirkland, WA 98033
(206) 827-9777

Baseball

Major League Baseball Player Association
805 Third Avenue
New York, NY 10022
(212) 826-0808

AMERICAN LEAGUE

American League Office
350 Park Avenue
New York, NY 10022
(212) 339-7600

Baltimore Orioles
Oriole Park at Camden Yards
333 W. Camden Street
Baltimore, MD 21201
(410) 243-9800

Boston Red Sox
Fenway Park
Boston, MA 02215
(617) 267-9440

California Angels
Anaheim Stadium
Anaheim, CA 92803
(714) 937-7200

Chicago White Sox
Comiskey Park
Chicago, IL 60616
(312) 924-1000

Cleveland Indians
Cleveland Stadium
Cleveland, OH 44114
(216) 861-1200

Detroit Tigers
Tiger Stadium
Detroit, MI 48216
(313) 962-4000

Kansas City Royals
Box 419969
Kansas City, MO 64141
(816) 921-2200

Milwaukee Brewers
Milwaukee County Stadium
Milwaukee, WI 53214
(414) 933-4114

Minnesota Twins
Hubert H. Humphrey Metrodome
Minneapolis, MN 55415
(612) 375-1366

New York Yankees
Yankee Stadium
Bronx, NY 10451
(212) 293-4300

Oakland Athletics
Oakland-Alameda County Coliseum
Oakland, CA 94621
(510) 638-4900

Seattle Mariners
Box 4100
Seattle, WA 98104
(206) 628-3555

Texas Rangers
Box 90111
Arlington, TX 76004
(817) 273-5222

Toronto Blue Jays
SkyDome
300 Brenner Blvd., Suite 3200
Toronto, Ontario, M5V 3B3 CAN
(416) 341-1000

NATIONAL LEAGUE:

Atlanta Braves
Box 4064
Atlanta, GA 30302
(404) 522-7630

Chicago Cubs
Wrigley Field
Chicago, IL
(312) 404-2827

Cincinnati Reds
Riverfront Stadium
Cincinnati, OH 45202
(513) 421-4510

Colorado Rockies
1700 Broadway, Suite 2100
Denver, CO 80203
(303) 866-0428

Florida Marlins
100 N.E. 3rd Avenue
Fort Lauderdale, FL 33301
(305) 779-7070

Houston Astros
Box 288
Houston, TX
(713) 799-9500

Los Angeles Dodgers
Dodger Stadium
Los Angeles, CA 90012
(213) 224-1500

Montreal Expos
Box 500, Station M
Montreal, Quebec, H1V 3P2 CAN
(514) 253-3434

National League Office
350 Park Avenue
New York, NY 10022
(212) 339-7700

New York Mets
Shea Stadium
Flushing, NY 11368
(718) 507-6387

Philadelphia Phillies
Box 7575
Philadelphia, PA 19101
(215) 463-6000

Pittsburgh Pirates
Box 7000
Pittsburgh, PA 15212
(412) 323-5000

St. Louis Cardinals
Busch Stadium
St. Louis, MO 63102
(314) 421-3060

San Diego Padres
Box 2000
San Diego, CA 92112
(619) 283-7294

San Francisco Giants
Candlestick Park
San Francisco, CA 94124
(415) 468-3700

Other Sports Associations

Afro-American Hall of Fame
149 California
Highland Park, Michigan 48203
(313) 345-5621

Association for Women in Sports Media
PO Box 4206
Millani, Hawaii 96789

Association of Black Sporting Goods Professionals
PO Box 83459
Los Angeles, California 90083
(310) 821-6910

Women's Sports Foundation
Eisenhower Park
East Meadow, New York 11554
(516) 542-4700

Sports Market Place
PO Box 1417
Princeton, New Jersey 08542
(609) 921-8599

INDEX

BOOKS OF AFRICAN-AMERICAN INTEREST

__INSIDE CORPORATE AMERICA: A GUIDE FOR
  AFRICAN AMERICANS
by Wilson Simmons III 0-399-51983-1/$12.00
Advice from a successful African-American businessman on everything
from interviews and internships to racism and office politics.

__TIMELINES OF AFRICAN-AMERICAN HISTORY:
  500 YEARS OF BLACK ACHIEVEMENT by Tom Cowan,
  Ph.D. and Jack Maguire 0-399-52127-5/$15.00
The first book to document the tumultuous, inspiring history of
African Americans—from the arrival of the first African explorers in
the 15th century to recent accomplishments of prominent African
Americans.

__THE GOLDEN THIRTEEN: RECOLLECTIONS OF
  THE FIRST BLACK NAVAL OFFICERS
  edited by Paul Stillwell 0-425-14373-2/$15.00
The United States Navy's first active duty African-American officers
recall how each maintained his dignity, pride, and humor to fight
prejudice while becoming pioneers in military history and role
models for all Americans.

__THE AFRICAN-AMERICAN ADDRESS BOOK
  by Tabatha Crayton 0-399-52148-8/$14.00
The first authoritative source of its kind, this book gives readers
access to the addresses of leading African-American citizens in
politics, the arts, business, culture, medicine, sports, and more.

__A ROCK AGAINST THE WIND: AFRICAN-AMERICAN
  POEMS AND LETTERS OF LOVE AND PASSION
  edited by Lindsay Patterson 0-399-51982-3/$12.00
Spanning generations, from the words of Langston Hughes to Maya
Angelou, a powerful collection of more than 100 African-American
love poems and letters.

Payable in U.S. funds. No cash orders accepted. Postage & handling: $1.75 for one book, 75¢ for each additional.
Maximum postage $5.50. Prices, postage and handling charges may change without notice. Visa, Amex,
MasterCard call 1-800-788-6262, ext. 1, refer to ad # 619a

Or, check above books and send this order form to: The Berkley Publishing Group 390 Murray Hill Pkwy., Dept. B East Rutherford, NJ 07073	Bill my: ☐ Visa ☐ MasterCard ☐ Amex expires _____
	Card#_____
	($15 minimum)
	Signature_____
Please allow 6 weeks for delivery.	Or enclosed is my: ☐ check ☐ money order
Name_____	Book Total $_____
Address_____	Postage & Handling $_____
City_____	Applicable Sales Tax $_____ (NY, NJ, PA, CA, GST Can.)
State/ZIP_____	Total Amount Due $_____